Explanation of Cover Design

Stone carving depicting sacred animal god and ear of corn

DESIGN FROM BOWL OF THE MIMBRES TYPE

Subject: three hunters following trail of a deer(?); hunters, probably dressed in skin jackets, carry bows and arrows and possibly throwing sticks. About A.D. 1100 to 1200.

Drawing taken from Figure 13, Archaeology of Mimbres Valley, by J. Walter Fewkes, Smithsonian Misc. Collections, vol. 63, no. 10.

Digging into History

A Brief Account of Fifteen Years of
Archaeological Work in New Mexico

BY

PAUL S. MARTIN

CHIEF CURATOR, DEPARTMENT OF ANTHROPOLOGY

Drawings by GUSTAF DALSTROM
ARTIST, DEPARTMENT OF ANTHROPOLOGY

CHICAGO NATURAL HISTORY MUSEUM

POPULAR SERIES

ANTHROPOLOGY, NUMBER 38

Preface

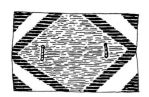

The purpose of this book is to piece together all the bits of the Mogollon Indian jigsaw puzzle that we discovered in New Mexico in our fifteen years of digging there. We gleaned a lot of odd facts and artifacts during that period, but they begin to shape up a vast and exciting picture of five thousand years of human history. My hope, here, is to connect these pieces in an orderly manner, and yet to infuse them with at least some of the dynamic overtones we all experienced during these years of discoveries.

But when a specialist writes for a lay audience, he finds himself in almost insurmountable difficulties of terminology. In my profession—as in all others, I presume—there is much jargon that is difficult to "translate." Sometimes it comes out in bewildering circumlocution! In a number of cases, therefore, I have retained relatively unfamiliar words, accompanied by explanations.

Writing this brief book has, in itself, been an adventure, and I hope the reader will be able to share it with me.

I wish to thank President Stanley Field, the Board of Trustees, and Dr. Clifford C. Gregg, Director of the Museum, for their generous financial support and personal interest in our archaeological research in the Southwest. This book would not have been possible without their sustained assistance.

Paul S. Martin

Contents

Headings and end-pieces represent pieces of pottery, stone tools, a Katchina, a portion of a tablita, an animal effigy, a "sun symbol," and designs from pottery.

Prologue

This book deals with the history of a "lost" tribe of Indians who lived long ago in western New Mexico. It will attempt to tell you what we have found out about the origin of these Indians, their development, changes that took place over thousands of years in their lives, the kinds of houses they built, and the kinds of crops they grew.

Columbus usually receives the credit for discovering the New World, but this honor should be given to migrants from northeastern Asia, whom we call the American Indians.

Detailed studies of the physical (racial) aspects of the American Indians show that they are all essentially Mongoloids, although there is some diversity among the various tribes of North, Middle and South America. This may be due to the fact that the American continent was interpenetrated (via Bering Strait) by successive groups of Asiatic migrants. These may have represented a composite of several racial strains, but primarily they were Mongoloid. In other words, some of the divergences of physical types, now observable in the Indians, first appeared in Asia and were then preserved in the New World.

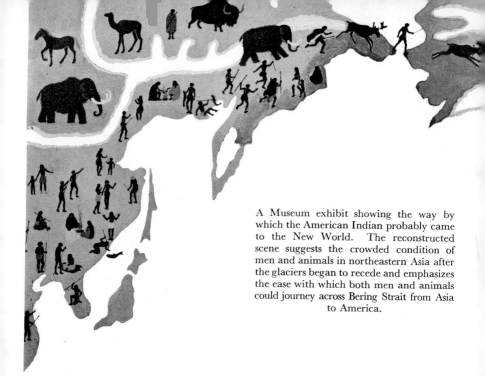

A Museum exhibit showing the way by which the American Indian probably came to the New World. The reconstructed scene suggests the crowded condition of men and animals in northeastern Asia after the glaciers began to recede and emphasizes the ease with which both men and animals could journey across Bering Strait from Asia to America.

Since no possible ancestral forms of modern man have ever been found in the New World, we may be sure that man did not originate here. Furthermore, since the American Indian may certainly be classed as belonging to the Mongoloid branch that originated in the Old World, we may be confident that he came from Asia. How he came and when and why are fascinating questions about which we have some information and some guesses. We guess that he entered by the easiest and shortest route and that would have been by Bering Strait, for here the distance between the Old and New Worlds is a mere sixty miles at the present time. If man started drifting into the New World about 25,000 years ago, it is safe to assume that he walked from Asia to America on dry land, for the two continents were connected by a land bridge. Even in much later times, when the land connection between the two continents was broken, man could have crossed by boat or on ice for the strait was narrower and shallower then.

The date of the earliest migrations from Asia to America cannot be exactly stated at present. It is safe to say, however, that man was present in the New World at least 25,000 years ago.

CONTINENTAL GLACIER
ICE 3 MILES THICK

A few migrants to the New World may have reached our shores by boat from the Pacific Islands, but it is usually conceded that such voyages were few in number and probably came about as a matter of chance rather than by intention. Furthermore, if such accidental voyagers lived to tell the tale, they and most of their specialized knowledge, traits, and techniques probably were largely, if not entirely, submerged by the civilization of their hosts.

There are speculations concerning the origin of the American Indians—such fables as Atlantis; The Lost Continent of Mu; the "lost" tribes of Israelites who were merely deported about 725 B.C. to Assyria and who may be described as displaced, enslaved and shuffled about, but *not* lost; and the like; but all of these "hypotheses" may be labeled as fiction based on fancies, opinions, and chance analogies.

The consensus of most anthropologists today is that the Indian is an Asiatic who wandered into the New World and here independently developed an impressive series of cultures that range from a modest set of attainments to higher civilization.

9

EXAMPLES OF EARLIEST AMERICANS

There is little doubt that the Asian emigrants, hereafter referred to as the American Indians, came unknowingly to the New World in pursuit of big game—the cold-steppe bison, the horse, the wooly mammoth, the musk-ox. These early hunters, armed with elaborate projectile weapons and excellent projectiles of flint, and aided by the cooperation and interest of the whole tribe, were sensibly following the well-marked trails left by these large, grazing animals. As would be expected, the trails led to grassy glades, water, and salt-licks and, as Dr. Loren Eisely (see Bibliography) points out, ran through mountain passes or across the lowest divides of the mountain ranges. The first comers were very smart to follow these trails.

This guess as to what kind of folk these earliest Americans were fits in very well with our bits of knowledge of the first Indians. It seems fairly certain from several well-explored sites that man's tools, garbage, camp sites, and earliest hearths (all spoken of as *cultural remains*) were associated with remains of now extinct large game.

I shall mention briefly three of these *finds* (for more details see the Bibliography: Luis Aveleyra, M. R. Harrington, E. W. Haury).

(1) At and near Tule Springs, in southern Nevada, Dr. M. R. Harrington, Mr. Fenley Hunter, and others discovered the camp ground of some of the early Indians. There they found bones of the mammoth, the American camel, the long-horned bison, deer, and two extinct species of American horses. Most of these bones had been split and charred, and in one fire-pit were the remains of a camel that had been cooked. Only two stone tools have been found associated with these remains: a crudely chipped tool of obsidian and one roughly made side-scraper.

The charcoal from the fire-pits was dated by the carbon 14 method as being 23,800 years old or perhaps more (see p. 53).

This is our earliest dated site up to the moment.

(2) Another example of a big animal that was successfully hunted for food by early American Indians comes from near Naco, in southern Arizona, southwest of Bisbee. Here Dr.

10

Emil Haury and Mr. E. B. Sayles found the remains of a Columbian mammoth killed by hunters who hurled eight stone spear-points into it. One of them, at least, pierced the animal's most vulnerable area—the spinal cord near the base of the skull. The hunters apparently hacked off the much-sought-after steaks and roasts and left the remainder of the carcass and the eight projectile points; eventually they were covered by sand and fill. The spear-points were of the type called Clovis Fluted.

Geologists think that this kill took place more than 10,000 years ago. The exact date cannot be determined at present, but one may guess that the ancient hunting party took place 12,000 to 20,000 years ago.

(3) An excellent account of a mammoth "find" in Mexico accompanied by three artifacts of stone, two spear-points and one knife, was described by Dr. Luis Aveleyra (see Bibliography).

AFFILIATIONS BETWEEN THESE EARLY HUNTERS AND THE EARLIEST MOGOLLON PEOPLE

Our story starts with the Cochise Indians who settled in southern Arizona about 6000 B.C. Their earliest history has has been partly reconstructed by archaeologists and geologists who have studied the ancient camp sites in which hearthstones, charcoal, tools of stone, and bones of extinct animals were found. Southern Arizona is now a desert, but it was cool and moist at that time and there were hickory and other trees that like relatively moist places. The region abounded in lakes and streams that were probably dammed up by beavers. Here the Cochise Indians hunted animals that are now extinct—the dire wolf, the American camel, the American horse, and the mammoth. The people camped along streams and lake shores and subsisted on nuts, seeds, berries, roots, and edible plants, supplementing this diet by some animal foods. Such a way of life is called a food-gathering economy because emphasis was on plant foods rather than on hunting. Agriculture, architecture, and pottery-making were unknown to these people.

11

MAP OF PINE LAWN VALLEY AND ADJACENT AREAS

For about 3,000 years the Cochise Indians went along in more or less the same manner. Tools changed and improved, but food-gathering plus some hunting remained the subsistence pattern. Dwellings may have been skin tents. The climate and environment were slowly changing, however. The continental glaciers were receding, lakes and streams were drying up, and the area was slowly becoming a desert. The large food animals were gradually becoming extinct.

It must have been plain to the Indians that their very existence was endangered, and this realization probably produced an era of unrest, peril, insecurity, and apprehension. The mental torture of the Cochise Indians must have been like our feelings today in the atomic age. At any rate, they had to move or perish, and some of them migrated northward, about 5,000 years ago (3000 b.c.) to Pine Lawn Valley in western New Mexico. This move brought the first settlers into the Valley. From their simple way of life grew a culture that lasted thousands of years and had important effects on neighboring peoples.

Once arrived, these Indians camped along a pleasant streamlet that issued from a spring high up in the nearby mountains. Living near a clear mountain stream must have been refreshing: water was always at hand for domestic purposes and for sustaining usable rushes and edible plants; water in quiet pools provided drinking places for deer, wild pig, bear, and other animals. The Indians resumed their old way of life—gathering wild seeds, nuts and roots which they ground up on stone slabs or milling stones; cleaning skins with roughly formed scrapers of stone; and chopping brush and firewood with heavy stone hand axes or choppers.

FIRST AGRICULTURE, HOUSES AND POTTERY

In the new homeland they also developed several new, worth-while ideas and inventions.

The idea of *planting seeds* was probably not difficult for the people to accept because for thousands of years they had watched plants grow, had gathered in their yield of edible bits, and may even have partly protected a few of their favorite

13

and most succulent shoots and herbs. At any rate, about 3000 to 4000 B.C., when the revolutionary conception of planting, cultivating, and guarding seeds of a new and mysterious plant-food that we call maize or corn was presented to the Cochise, they were ready to accept such an idea. Thus was agriculture established and a blessing it was, for with a more assured food supply less time and less effort had to be spent in searching for wild food plants. With less time expended on food-gathering, leisure increased and life became less tenuous, especially for the thrifty who put aside a surplus of the corn to tide themselves and their families over a season of drought. With leisure, they had a chance to develop arts and other skills; and with a stable food supply, the population tended to increase. Soon after the introduction of corn, which probably came from Mexico and ultimately perhaps from South America, beans and squash also were adopted from more southern peoples. By 2500 B.C., corn, beans, and squash were a part of the Cochise food supply.

Also, from some unknown source came the knowledge that men could live more comfortably in pit-houses. A pit-house is a neatly excavated hole from 12 to 20 feet in diameter and from 2 to 4 feet deep, over which a roof of poles, brush, and sod can be constructed.

Soon thereafter (surely about 300 B.C.), the Cochise borrowed from southerly neighbors the art of molding, polishing, coloring, and firing selected clays into containers, such as bowls and jars.

COCHISE CULTURE BECOMES MOGOLLON

Thus, shortly before the beginning of the Christian era— not later than 300 B.C.—the Cochise culture had been greatly modified and augmented. In aggregate these changes are so pronounced and significant that we have decided to mark this milepost of advance by bestowing another name on the new total. The term "Mogollon" has been adopted to signify the addition of agriculture, house-building, and pottery-making (and other customs to be discussed later). This term connotes one of the longest continuous cultural growths in North America, with roots reaching back to about 6000 B.C. and with

14

trunk, limbs, and leaves reaching perhaps up to the present time—a span of perhaps about 8,000 years.

It should be understood then, that the term "Mogollon" as used in this book means an extension and a ramification of the Cochise civilization. Cochise and Mogollon cultures may be regarded as a more or less single and continuous development. There is no break in our story at all, but there is a transition. To restate briefly: the Mogollon civilization is Cochise plus farming, pit-houses, pottery, a few new types of stone tools and other additions to be discussed in later sections.

Now we come back to the question posed at the beginning of this chapter: Are the early big-game hunters related to the Cochise Indians? Or to reverse the question: Can we claim the big-game hunters as ancestors of the Cochise and, in turn, of the Mogollon Indians? The answer is that at present we do not know. If the people at Naco, who killed the big mammoth, are the ancestors of the Cochise Indians, then we have to assume that they later radically modified their way of life to the extent of learning to place more dependence on the gathering of wild plants for food usage and of relying less on hunting. This change is theoretically possible; but actually there is a hiatus in our knowledge of what was happening in southern Arizona at 10,000 B.C. (the time of the Naco mammoth hunters) and 6000 B.C., the time of the earlier Cochise people.

We think now that the big game hunters were more characteristic of eastern, central, and northern North America. It may be that the Cochise people represent a different Asiatic group—one that had already "drifted" into a food-gathering economy with but slight dependence on game for food *before* coming to the New World.

The Cochise civilization is classified as belonging to a *Desert Culture* which was well adapted to its distinctive environment and was better able to cope with changing conditions than the early Indian big-game hunters. The Naco mammoth find, then, is, at present, regarded as evidence of an example of infrequent penetration by big-game hunters into the domain of the Cochise peoples, who, in turn, developed into the pottery-using, crop-growing Indians that we call Mogollon.

15

The gulf between us and the Mogollon people is a large one and difficult to span. It is not easy to write about people who lived so many years ago and make them appear as human beings. The characters of the cast are different from us and the setting is an unusual one. But the story is a human record in which we note large accomplishments by means of details. As one man puts it, most people are commonplace, and their lives, lived out in the prosaic middle register between saint and sinner, make up the real meat and marrow of the world.

We do not know what these people called themselves but we call them the Mogollon Indians (pronounced Mog-ee-yown) and their very existence was not actually known until about twenty years ago. It is interesting to note, however, that about fifty years ago an archaeologist from the United States National Museum suspected, on the basis of evidence that he found in what we call the Upper Gila Valley, that is, the area in which we have been digging in west central New Mexico, that the material remains—the pottery, the houses, the bone tools, the stone tools, and the like—were not the same as those found in northern New Mexico and Arizona. He thought that they were, perhaps, made by a different people who came from or lived southward. We now know that the guess was correct.

Brief SKETCHES

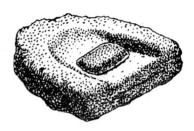

of SOUTHWESTERN CULTURE

This story will be limited to a branch or subdivision of the Southwestern Indians—the Mogollones. A little background of the other Southwestern cultures will be given first.

INTRODUCTION

Archaeological interest in the Southwestern part of the United States—that is, Arizona, New Mexico, and parts of Nevada, Utah and Colorado—began in 1875 or thereabouts. At that time the country was being settled by cattlemen, sheepmen, and farmers. The large standing ruins that were fairly abundant in parts of Arizona, New Mexico, and Colorado naturally attracted the interest of lay workers as well as that of archaeologists. From about 1880 to 1910 many famous scientists visited the Southwest and described numerous sites and the Indians they saw there. From about 1875 to 1925, it was commonly believed by most laymen and most archaeologists that the entire area had been inhabited and developed by one group, the so-called Pueblo people. The great cliffhouses at Mesa Verde, the large, open, D-shaped villages in Chaco Canyon, the famous villages in southwestern New Mex-

17

ico that produced beautiful pottery, the great adobe houses of southern Arizona, the canals in that area, and all the villages and pueblos and ruins of all kinds up and down the Gila, the Salt, the Little Colorado, and the San Juan Rivers—all of these were supposed to have been the work of the Pueblo Indians. We now know that this was a very simplified picture of what had actually occurred. At the present time archaeologists recognize four major subdivisions and four major subcultures of the Southwest. Each of these major subdivisions and sub-cultures had characteristics of its own and for some time it was believed that each flourished independently. Recent work has shown that each did have its own individual characteristics, but that all of them are united in various subtle but tangible ways. All these four sub-cultures seem to have been motivated by similar impulses to change in more or less the same directions at about the same time. And all reached a climax about A.D. 1300. It is as if the area had been washed over several times by waves of similar cultural influences.

The names of the four major sub-cultures are: (1) Anasazi; (2) Hohokam; (3) Mogollon; and (4) Patayan.

THE ANASAZI CULTURE *inclusive of Basketmaker, Cliff Dwellers, Pueblos,*

The word "Anasazi"—which is an Anglicized version of the Navaho term meaning "old people"—is the name now applied to Basketmakers, Cliff Dwellers, and Pueblo Indians. Anasazi, then, is the inclusive term.

The territory in which the Anasazi Indians lived from about the beginning of the Christian era is what is known today as the "Four-Corners" region. This region may be roughly described as northeastern Arizona, northwestern New Mexico, southeastern Utah and southwestern Colorado. Anasazi ruins are found from Flagstaff eastward to the Rio Grande River, but the concentration is mostly in the "Four-Corners" area. Even today there are remnants of the Anasazi people living in or about the same area; for example, the Hopi Indians live in northeastern Arizona, the Zuñi Indians live in towns close to the Arizona–New Mexico border, and the

18

Rio Grande Indians live in and around Albuquerque and Santa Fe. All of these present-day Indians have retained a remarkable degree of their ancient culture, and the Zuñi and Hopi Indians are noted for their conservatism because they have effectively resisted the encroachments of our European civilization.

The Anasazi civilization which flourished on the Colorado plateau of the Intermontane division has been more intensively investigated and written about than any of the others. For fifty years, reports, monographs, articles, and stories have been pouring from the pens of various authors, and the literature is very voluminous. Therefore, I shall condense what I have to say about this culture. Briefly, it may be summed up as follows:

Taking Anasazi culture as a whole from beginning to end, without differentiating the time factors, we may say that its chief characteristics are (1) masonry; (2) agglomerations of houses, often several stories high (roughly similar to our clusters of rooms called apartment houses); (3) the kiva, or ceremonial underground chamber; (4) altars; (5) sand paintings (ritualistic scenes portrayed free-hand with sands of various colors); (6) priestly offices; (7) elaborate rituals and symbolisms, some of which were secret and celebrated in the sanctuary (kiva) and many of which were held in the open for the enjoyment and inspiration of the entire village; (8) special public dances performed by katchinas or representatives of the gods to re-enact the Hopi beliefs concerning the origin of the tribe and to insure peace, prosperity, rainfall, good crops, tribal fertility, and health, and to express thankfulness for past favors; (9) probably mother-line descent; (10) textured or corrugated grayish cooking pottery; (11) decorated pottery with a gray or white background and designs in black paint; (12) decorated pottery of a polychrome and glazed decorated type.

The Anasazi culture, like the other three sub-cultures, grew by continuous transitions and additions and accretions from an ancient and widespread culture called the Desert Culture of the Great Basin (the Intermontane area). The Desert Culture came into existence some 11,000 years ago and monopolized most of the territory in the Great Basin—that is, from Oregon and Idaho southward through Nevada, Utah, and parts of California and Colorado, Arizona, and New Mexico—and extended into the northern part of Mexico. The Great Basin area lies mostly within the sagebrush-juniper-pinyon zone, although there are good-sized regions of short desert grass and of pines, hemlocks, and spruce in the higher mountains. Parenthetically, it is interesting to note that today most of the area is occupied by peoples who speak dialects of the Uto-Aztecan language, including the modern Hopis, Pimas, Utes, Paiutes and Shoshones, and some of the Rio Grande Indians.

Most of the later and so-called higher developments of the Anasazi came to them from the Hohokam and Mogollon groups (see below), so that the climax that occurred about A.D. 1100 may be regarded as an accumulation of southern and possibly Mexican traits that were taken over by the Anasazi bit by bit—by trade, by drift, perhaps by war—and reworked to fit their ideas and cultural layout. In fact, much of the great efflorescence of culture that took place in the Hopi and Zuñi towns may be due to ideas conceived by the Mogollon peoples who were beginning to move up into the Hopi-Zuñi country around 1200 to 1300.

THE HOHOKAM CULTURE

Now let us look briefly at the Hohokam culture. The civilization of the Hohokam Indians (Hohokam is an anglicized version of the Pima Indian term meaning "that which has perished"), like that of the Anasazi, was probably derived from a desert culture that was established some 11,000 years ago in the Intermontane region. The area of Hohokam specialization lay mostly along the Gila River and its tributaries in the southern half of Arizona—that is, in the desert regions of Phoenix and Tucson. Hohokam features and villages are found, however, far beyond this limited area. Certainly Hohokam traits spread as far north as the Flagstaff region and as far south as the international border—perhaps even farther.

As I stated above, the Gila–Salt River drainages, now known to be the homeland of the Hohokam, were formerly

20

considered a part of the Puebloan Southwest. Prior to 1920 every archaeological site in the Southwest was dubbed "cliff-dweller" or "Pueblo." In short, the Southwest was "the Pueblo area." A few imaginative archaeologists who heeded the evidence thought otherwise. The great contrast between the materials found in the Gila River desert ruins and those from the Plateau sites made them think that perhaps it was a bit "fishy" to lump together two obviously different groups. The trouble is that they had no concrete evidence on which to base sound deductions.

But, thanks to Gila Pueblo at Globe, Arizona (a privately endowed research institution, supported and directed by Mr. and Mrs. H. S. Gladwin, but now dissolved, alas), work was carried on in the fall, winter, and spring seasons. Due entirely to the dogged persistence of the Gladwins and their staff, the Gila desert area and the territories surrounding it—east, west, south, and north—were systematically explored. By 1928 or 1929, the staff of Gila Pueblo knew for certain that the Gila–Salt River drainages and the desert area were *not* parts of the Pueblo area and that the archaeological remains represented a separate entity or sub-culture. Thus they discovered the Hohokam civilization. The Pueblo "one world" was shattered, and about 1930, or thereabouts, Southwestern archaeologists conceded that the Southwest geographical area embraced several prehistoric civilizations. The acceptance of the Mogollon culture as another entity was delayed for several years. Scientific explorations and excavations in Hohokam sites has not yet been extensive, but each year sees more work done in this interesting civilization. Enough is now known, however, so that we can describe confidently the high lights of the Hohokam sub-culture. The largest site, Snaketown, was investigated for several seasons by the staff of Gila Pueblo.

If we take the Hohokam civilization from early to late (from about the beginning of the Christian era to about A.D. 1400) without regard to time periods, we may list its traits as follows: (1) pit-houses—structures with the floor below the surface of the ground, and the roof made of brush and mud (note: storied clusters of houses were never built by the Hohokam); (2) villages composed of scattered houses, but no

21

towns; (3) compound walls around some of the later villages; (4) irrigation ditches for taking water from the Gila and its tributaries to the fields (without irrigation of some type agriculture would have been impossible in this desert); (5) pottery made by the paddle and anvil process instead of the coiling process used by the Anasazi and Mogollon Indians, and manufactured in such a way as to produce a red ware or a buff type with designs in red paint (red-on-buff ware); (6) etched shell ornaments; (7) excellent stone carvings; (8) well-made projectile points; (9) stone axes of fine quality, the handles of which were fastened to a three-quarter groove (a groove that runs around three sides of the tool); (10) rituals that were probably simpler than and different from the complex ones of the Anasazi; (11) ball courts in which a kind of ceremonial basketball game was played; (12) small kivas; (13) medicine men rather than priests and a priesthood; (14) father-line descent; (15) perhaps some aggressiveness or warlike expansive traits.

What became of the Hohokam peoples after A.D. 1400? Did they and their civilization perish from the face of the earth? Several anthropologists have conjectured that the modern Pima Indians who live in southern Arizona are the cultural descendants of the Hohokam Indians, and recent work by the Amerind Foundation of Arizona has strengthened this hypothesis. If this is so, then we have an unbroken continuity of the Hohokam culture from a desert base of about 11,000 years ago, through the Hohokam civilization itself, which surely came into being by the beginning of the Christian era, right down to the present Pima or related Indians. In other words, the Hohokam civilization faltered and changed its course and thereby lost much of its polish about A.D. 1400, but it did not perish.

There are many differences between the traits of the Anasazi and Hohokam Indians. Chief among these are: For the Anasazi: masonry; storied houses with clustered rooms; "towns;" the kiva; priests and altars; grayish plain or black-on-white pottery and, later, black-on-yellow or orange wares and glazed paint wares. For the Hohokam: lack of masonry; pit-houses; small groups of houses; the compound; the ball

22

court; shamans rather than a priesthood; and red-on-buff
pottery that cannot compare for general excellence with the
Anasazi ceramics.

medicine-men

The Mogollon culture, as noted above, was also discovered by the staff of Gila Pueblo in 1934 or thereabouts. The
first excavations in a Mogollon site were made by Dr. Emil W.
Haury, whose publication is now a landmark in the archaeological works of the Southwest. But for a long time conservative archaeologists refused to accept the Mogollon civilization
as a separate entity. Now, however, this culture stands on its
own feet and has been accepted by archaeologists throughout
the world. No more at this point will be said about it.

THE PATAYAN CULTURE

The fourth sub-culture of the Southwest is called Patayan
(with accent on the second syllable). It is the least studied and
described of the four principal civilizations of the Southwest.
The name, Patayan, is taken from the Yuman language and
the word means "ancient people." The dates for this culture
are at the moment tentatively placed at A.D. 700 to 1100.
A few good excavations have been carried on in Patayan sites,
and from these studies, together with the vast amount of information gleaned from "surveys" carried on by the Museum
of Northern Arizona, we can derive some tentative conclusions.

The Patayans are believed to be the cultural, physical and
linguistic ancestors of the present-day Havasupai, Walapai, or
Yuman tribes, who occupy much of the same territory on the
Colorado River plateau and in the canyons of that river as did
the ancient Patayan. In ancient times these Indians lived
not only along the Colorado River but also as far east as the
Verde River at Flagstaff and south approximately as far as
34° N. Lat.

The ancient economy of the Patayan Indians was probably
based on agriculture plus some hunting and food-gathering.
Thus it resembles the other three sub-cultures. Houses were
of several types and were probably occupied seasonally—possibly a snug type of earth-covered, dome-shaped house for
winter habitation, and a "shade" structure for summer usage.

23

Villages as such did not exist; houses were scattered singly over a general area. Stone tools such as the lower and upper parts of corn-grinding stones (metates and manos), projectile points, knives and scrapers occur but were not of noteworthy workmanship. No religious structures or burials have been found.

In general, one senses that the Patayans farmed sporadically and where they could; expressed little interest in manufacturing tools of bone and stone; made few or no ornaments; and left behind no ceremonial structures of the type that is usually regarded as evidence of a visible ritual, such as the Anasazi possessed. This does not necessarily mean a lack of religious ideas; perhaps their religion was expressed in other ways. All in all, the Patayan culture shows some resemblances to, or at least an indirect relationship with, the ancient and widespread cultures of the Great Basin. Here again it resembles the other three sub-cultures. There are also connections with later Anasazi civilizations, but these are regarded as due to borrowing.

This concludes the brief discussion of the four different sub-cultures of the southwestern part of the United States. I have stressed their differences in order to make clear to the reader that each has reality and that each can be distinguished from the other. Now I wish to point out the hypothesis that these four sub-cultures are intimately related in one way or another even though each has its own distinct flavor. That is why I prefer the term "sub-culture" for each one, so that the emphasis is placed on the fact that the Southwest is one large "culture area." A culture area may be roughly defined as a geographical region that embraces similar or related culture traits or elements, similar patterns and drifts that must be regarded as having depth in time. The Southwest culture area appears, then, to comprise four related but consistently distinctive culture types or sub-cultures.

Thus I believe that the Southwest can be regarded or characterized as a natural culture area that is a distinctive one. The four sub-cultures, considered collectively, certainly stand in stark contrast to those of the west, north, and east. This

24

concept emphasizes the similarities that exist among the four local sub-cultures among which there has been an interchange of cultural factors and ideas. By this concept we sweep aside the artificial boundaries that archaeologists have thought up between the various groups (Anasazi, Hohokam, and the like), and point out that there probably was a large degree of mobility and interchange of ideas throughout the entire Southwest in all times—that is, from about 11,000 years ago down to the moment. That is what I mean by time depth.

INTERRELATIONSHIPS BETWEEN THE FOUR SUB-CULTURES

This concept of interrelationships, sometimes called the "area co-tradition," stresses the intimacy that existed between tribes, groups, and villages. By creating this thing that might be called a "cultural abstraction"—that is, an entity that is more inclusive and on a higher plane of thinking than merely looking at pottery, tools, baskets, and sandals from various sub-cultures and stating that these are "different" and independently made—we are able to cut away the underbrush of details and look at the Southwest as a homogeneous area made up of traits many of which have a common origin.

On this homogeneous base, the four sub-cultures grew and developed in various ways; but we can also see that the four allied and more or less parallel developments were "different" and yet attained a remarkable and uniform development throughout the entire region. For example, the Southwest, in contrast to the Plains area or the regions eastward toward and beyond the Mississippi River, may be called a "painted pottery" area. We can note a tendency for parallel development of the sequences of pottery designs throughout the area and through time. By this I mean that the designs on the painted pottery for the four sub-groups gradually shift from early to late—from large simple bowls with broad-lined designs, to finer-lined, more complex layouts and designs. Thus we can see in pottery, as well as in architecture, tools, baskets, art forms and the like, a greater historical intimacy between the four sub-cultures than between any or all of them and the cultures of the Mississippi Valley. We can observe a general

25

cultural *drift* in Southwestern cultures similar to that which can be observed and corroborated in linguistics.

In language there is *drift;* that is, language is constantly, though slowly, changing and shifting according to certain patterns and in a consistent direction. No language is ever static. The rules for governing drift in Indo-European languages are not the same as those for Asiatic or American Indian languages. Under primitive conditions, we can guess that political groups are small, and thus dialects arise. In time, these dialects and people, perhaps, drift apart so much that there is differentiation. Then dialects split up into sub-dialects. To illustrate from Sapir, the great American linguist, it is fairly certain that languages so little resembling one another as modern Irish, English, Italian, Greek, Russian, Armenian, Persian, and Bengali are but end-points of drifts that converge to a meeting point in the far past. A very simple example of the tendency for language to change may be seen in the modern phrase, "who did you see?"—instead of "whom did you see?" In a few centuries or less "whom" will be as obsolete as "thou."

This is a very brief and simplified explanation of a complex phenomenon. But the point is that culture and all parts of culture—that is, architecture, pottery, basketry, art forms, social organization and language—drift according to certain patterns and in a consistent direction of which the individual culture-bearer is unaware.

The four sub-cultures of the Southwest—Anasazi, Hohokam, Mogollon, Patayan—probably sprang from a common base, as explained earlier, and have drifted somewhat apart so that each looks different or unique, if you will. But actually, all of them are interrelated, just as, very roughly, modern English and Armenian languages are related.

Thus the cultures of the Southwest may be thought of as one large unit which can best be compared with other substantial units of culture history elsewhere in the world. Cultural changes can be examined and their causes sought. This larger concept of interrelationships or the co-tradition may be useful, although we must not let it deter us from seeking the particulars of some local culture or from trying to understand

26

the growth of culture in restricted areas; that is, one has to have the detailed studies that contain many minutiae and descriptions of bone and stone tools, pottery, basketry, houses, and the like in order to form this wider concept. The complete understanding of any culture—and here the Mogollon in particular—requires that we use every available tool for understanding human development; and we must travel every pathway of exploration that we can find.

PURPOSES of WORK

in NEW MEXICO

WHY AND HOW WE DUG IN NEW MEXICO

We have spoken briefly of the origin of the American Indians and of when they came over to this country or to this
New World; now let us pause briefly to tell you a little bit
about the physical aspects of our work.

We chose to work in west central New Mexico, or the
Upper Gila area, located near Reserve, the county seat of
Catron County—a county that is almost as large as the state
of Massachusetts—because the Mogollon Indians who had
lived there presented rather an alluring history. Although
remains of these Indians had been discovered some five years
before we went into western New Mexico, very little work
had been done on the sites they had occupied. We spent
twelve summers there digging in sites of various types and
sizes, and then spent the winters working over the material
that we had dug up—analyzing it, sifting it, washing it and
thinking about it. We have now finished working in the area
and we wish to bring together for you the results of some of
our work and to tell you about some of the guesses we have
made concerning the Mogollon civilization.

HOW RUINS ARE FOUND

First let me tell you how our sites or villages are found, and how we decide which ones should be chosen for digging. When we move into a new area, the location of ancient destroyed or collapsed villages is difficult for us to find. We walk, we ride on horseback, we travel by car, we climb hills and ridges, and descend into arroyos or gullies, and while we are thus traversing the country up and down or horizontally we are constantly examining the ground, looking for the evidences of ancient villages. At first the Mogollon villages were difficult for us to find, but after we had been there a little time we learned that the early sites were usually up on almost unscalable mesas, or near springs that flowed high up in the mountains, and that the later villages were usually lower down, along ancient stream beds or near modern rivers. We spent several seasons looking for sites, but we located some 185 ancient villages. For each one we made a record telling of its location, so that we could go back to it again, and noting the kind of pottery that was lying on the ground and the kind of stone tools that were cast about. The earliest villages or camp sites were the very hardest to find because they were inhabited before pottery was made. Therefore, we had to depend on other kinds of evidence for detecting these ancient sites—broken stone tools of various kinds, an ancient hearth or fireplace that had been exposed by recent erosion, or sometimes a shallow saucer-shaped depression from 12 to 18 feet across. These saucer-shaped depressions were the remains of pit-houses. The broken stone tools were milling stones (that is, stones that were used for grinding up nuts, berries and corn); pieces of spear points made of obsidian and quartz; large, crudely flaked stones that were the axes or choppers of the day; pestles; scrapers; and even mortars. But all these tools were made of stone and all were necessary to a people who were depending at that time more on wild plants than on animals for food. The later villages, usually located, as I said earlier, near or on the floors of river valleys, can immediately be spotted because they are piles of rocks in disorder. These rocks represent compact villages of contiguous rooms, that is, rooms that are wall to wall as they are in our modern apart-

Archaeologists washing and classifying small pieces of pottery (potsherds)
found in the dig.

ment buildings. There may be as few as three or four rooms in the village or as many as 75 or 80. Scattered about these later habitations we find pieces of pottery known to archaeologists as potsherds, stone chips by the thousands strewn over several acres, and many pieces of broken tools representing milling or grinding tools, spear or arrow heads, choppers or axes, mortars, pestles, knives, and drills.

These sites, both early and late, that I have described, lie in the open, that is, right under the sky; but there is another kind of site that is of equal interest to us. We devoted several seasons to finding dry caves in which the Mogollon Indians had lived at one time or another. I speak of dry caves because, if a cave had been moist or wet at any time, all of the material made of cloth, plants, or wood—baskets, sandals, throwing sticks, bows and arrows, fur garments, or vegetable food remains—would have disintegrated or rotted away. We were lucky enough to find two dry caves and these we excavated. A wealth of material came out of these caves! Our major finds consisted of tools of bone and antler, objects of leather, of string, pieces of matting, baskets, sandals, cigarettes, bows, arrows, and other articles of substances usually considered perishable but which here, because of the extraordinary dryness in the caves, had been well preserved. After several years of intensive analysis of our materials, and with the help of other experts, we determined that one of these caves had been inhabited more or less continuously for 2,000 or more years.

HOW WE CHOOSE A SITE TO DIG

Now that I have told you how sites are found and how they look before the digging begins, I should explain how we choose which to dig; for of course we cannot dig all of the habitations or villages that we find.

Accessibility is one of the main factors in making a decision about an ancient site. If we are not able to drive reasonably close to our dig or if we are unable to construct a rough road that will bring us close to it, we usually do not attempt extensive excavations, for the simple reason that we may have to carry all of our tools, our water, our lunches, the camera, the

Archaeologists mapping a great kiva with surveyors' instruments.

photographic tower, and the like anywhere from two to four miles up and down hills. Thus, ease of approach is a factor.

We try to select a site or several sites that look promising and that will reveal the history of the Mogollon people at various periods in their development. I shall have to anticipate my conclusions and my dating, but I think it is safe to say that the Pine Lawn area in west central New Mexico, where we have been digging for the past fifteen years, was inhabited somewhere between 4,000 and 5,000 years. It was abandoned about A.D. 1350 or 1400. Since we knew from our survey and our card-records of the sites that we had a long span of human habitation in the area, we knew in advance that we should have to spend at least eight to twelve years digging in that area. We started with the earliest sites, and since they were so strange and since such as these had never before been excavated, we spent several seasons digging from 26 to 30 pit-houses. These pit-houses had been roofed over by means of pine logs which in turn had been covered with earth and sod; thus a fairly comfortable house had been created, a house that looked something like a gigantic ant hill.

Thus, in the twelve seasons we were there, we dug some 25 sites that represented from 4,000 to 5,000 years of history. The earliest sites would date at around 3500 B.C. and the latest at about A.D. 1350 to 1400.

Now, perhaps digging up "lost" civilizations may sound romantic, and in some ways it *is* exciting; but it is also composed mostly of hard work in dust, under a hot sun, amid swarms of insects, or it is carried on during showers of rain. Digging in a cave is even worse. Dust and heat are oppressive, and the wearing of masks and goggles—an uncomfortable and trying experience—is absolutely necessary to give the workmen protection from toxic dust.

Added to these discomforts is another—inadequate ventilation. The caves that we excavated in 1950 and in 1951 are small—about 40 feet deep by 30 feet wide at the mouth and 6 feet or less high. At the end of the day the workers looked as if they had been digging in a coal mine.

CAMP ROUTINE

Perhaps a word concerning our daily routine would be of interest. We leave camp about seven o'clock in a truck loaded with tools and workmen. The site may be as much as fifty miles away. Digging proceeds through the day unless rains are so violent that we cannot continue. At the end of the day the materials found are brought back to camp in sacks, each carefully marked with the exact location of the material it contains. In an open site, as noted above, our finds consist mostly of pottery or potsherds (if this site is late enough to produce

Archaeologists cataloging materials found in the dig.

pottery), tools of stone and bone, sometimes a skeleton or two, and, rarely, a bit of treasure in the form of painted stones used in ceremonies.

While work continues the next day at the dig, the specially trained workers at the camp process the materials brought in the preceding day. By "processing" I mean that all the pottery and potsherds are washed, sorted, classified and counted according to types. The stone and bone tools are also washed, classified and catalogued. At the end of a day the previous day's finds are completely taken care of. At the end of the camp season, the sherds and the bone and stone tools are all shipped back to the museum in Chicago. Then starts the long, delicate task of studying these remains very carefully so that we can come forth with conclusions about the life of these ancient people. Our conclusions are based always on facts, and from them we can make many guesses. Our historical reconstructions are founded on thousands of small details and bits of materials that were excavated and have been recorded with care; on common sense interpretations (a sharp, pointed, slender bone tool with an eye was probably used for sewing; charcoal found in a scooped-out pocket in the floor of an ancient house probably means that fire was maintained there by man for one or more purposes); and on some assumptions.

PUTTING THE PIECES TOGETHER

Thus we piece together our story—the history that I am going to relate in this book. It is based on many long hours of digging in dusty caves or in ruined houses that were built in the open, and after that comes the patient analysis of the meaning of all of these data. Since these people did not have any writing, we must depend on the remains of animals and plants, the architectural remains, bits of pottery, stone tools and the like for our reconstructions. From such evidence we can usually tell whether a given prehistoric people were hunters and fishermen or whether they were farmers. Sometimes we find that they hunted and gathered wild foods and farmed also.

The relationship of geography, climate and environment to culture or to civilization is a very important one and one that has to be studied with great care. One of the great advantages of the research that we have undertaken—a study that spans such a long period of time—is the opportunity it offers us to examine the ways in which people worked out their social needs and the ways in which they made a living. The making of a living by the Mogollon Indians was a definite adjustment to specific physical and biological conditions, based on certain needs, capacities and values. The character of the environment more or less influenced what these people could do. The study of the relationship between man and his environment and the development of his civilization viewed from these points gives us some idea of how much control man has over forces external to himself. The economy of any community is necessarily the product of an adjustment between

35

man and his environment. You cannot expect the Eskimo, living in his Arctic environment, to build houses of palm thatch; nor could you expect the Indians of the Southwest to build their houses of blocks of snow. These are very simple illustrations of what I mean. Let us look briefly at the environment and climate of the territory in which the Mogollon Indians lived for such a long period of time.

THE MOGOLLON HOMELAND

About 4,500 to 5,000 years ago the climate in the Pine Lawn area of west central New Mexico began slowly to change. For some three or four thousand years the region had been very warm and dry, but about 3000 to 2500 B.C. the climate became relatively cool and moist. When I say *relatively* cool and moist I mean compared to the previous period of some three thousand years. Even today the region is not blessed with a superabundance of moisture; for example, the rainfall in the Pine Lawn valley today is about 14 inches per year, whereas the average annual precipitation in the Chicago area is about 33 inches per year. Nevertheless, in spite of this relatively dry country, the Mogollon Indians flourished for a long time.

About 4,500 years ago a band or two of these Indians left their homes in the southern part of the area, which was gradually drying up, and moved northward. We do not think the early Mogollon nomads were given to straying here and there, or that they were driven out by other stronger Indians, or that they were filled with a desire to explore and seek new lands and fortunes. They were probably forced to depart from their homeland by the shrinking of the lakes and rivers near which they and their ancestors had lived for thousands of years. They may have dispersed in several directions, but certainly a handful—perhaps a hundred or more—discovered Pine Lawn valley. So far as we know, they were the first settlers of the valley, and from their simple way of life grew a culture that lasted many centuries and probably had important effects on neighboring peoples.

Once arrived at this pleasant valley that hugs the Arizona border in west central New Mexico, the Mogollon people

Interior of Tularosa Cave, looking from the trench
toward the entrance

Excavating a "mummy" in Tularosa Cave
(about A.D. 500)

camped along the banks of a streamlet that issued from a spring high up in the nearby mountains. The spring still flows. Living near a mountain stream must have been pleasant in many ways because the water was always at hand for domestic purposes, it sustained many usable rushes and edible plants, and it provided drinking places for deer, wild pig, bear, rabbits and other animals of the chase.

Geographically, the Mogollon homeland is among the roughest, most mountainous countries of the Southwest. In general, one might say that it lies south of the province of Colorado plateaus and is situated in what geographers call the Mexican Highlands section of the Basin and Range province. In this area there are several great mountain ranges—the White Mountains, the San Francisco Mountains, the Blue Mountains, and the Tularosa Mountains. The Little Colorado Plateau area, which lies north of this region, drains northwestward toward the Little Colorado River. The Mogollon area, which lies south of this, drains southwest entirely, into the Gila–Salt River system of rivers. Briefly, the terrain of the Mogollon country may be called the most cut-up area in the Southwest. It is probably also the best watered. Naturally, climate and vegetation and rainfall all vary according to the range in elevation. Farther south of the Mogollon area, in the desert, rainfall of course is very scanty. On the higher elevations, anywhere from 6,000 to 8,000 feet, grasslands are abundant and on the mountains are forests of pinyon, juniper, oak, pine, spruce, and Douglas fir. In spite of its great natural beauty and rugged character, the Mogollon area is not suitable for large-scale agriculture because the valleys are narrow and steep. The villages probably were concentrated where these valleys open out into broader, alluvial flats. One other feature should be pointed out, and that is that the valleys and canyons are somewhat cut off from one another and therefore make for isolation and corresponding development of sub-cultures within this area. We do not expect to find uniformity of cultural development in such a cut-up or dissected region. The people tended to move up and down the narrow valleys or streams and were probably shut off from contacts with other tribes by the high mountain masses. It might be of general interest to note that this uninhabited and inhospitable territory was crossed in 1539 by a Spanish leader, the Mareos de Nisa, and later by Coronado, who discovered or was told about the village of Zuñi, which still exists.

Screening dirt from Tularosa Cave to recover household goods, tools, clothing and food left by Mogollon Indians during 1500 to 2000 years of occupation.

Geologically, the region is composed of igneous formations of great variety. Cappings of extrusive basalt or lava that flowed out of nearby volcanoes cover all the earlier, softer rocks. On some of the plateaus large areas are covered with soil that lies fairly deep because of constant additions from what one might call temporary lakes. In the spring these areas are marshes. If there were more rainfall, many of these basins of the plateau country would be lakes.

CULTURAL ECOLOGY

The mineral resources of the area furnished a very abundant supply of rocks which were useful to the Indians in making tools and building fireplaces and houses. Furthermore, iron ores such as hematite and limonite were fairly abundant and these were used for paint in painting pottery, perhaps painting the human body in dances, and certainly in painting some ceremonial objects. Copper may be present, although I do not know this. In all the years that we have been digging and in all the thousands of cubic yards of dirt that we have moved, we have found only two copper specimens—a copper bell probably made in Mexico and imported to our area, and a copper object that may represent an animal.

Vegetable material was extremely abundant. The evergreen trees—pinyons and pines—furnished timber for building, that is, for roof logs and for bows; the oaks furnished firewood, and wood for clubs, for digging-sticks, and throwing-sticks; and some of the softer woods, like cottonwood, may have been used for making prayer-sticks. Shrubs and plants were plentiful, and were used for making basketry, mats, and sandals. Reeds were used for arrow-shafts, ceremonial offerings and flutes. Later on, corn, beans, squash, and gourds were grown, as well as cotton. Tobacco grew wild in the area and was smoked. The wild plants furnished a large proportion of the daily diet and in early times perhaps the greater part—walnuts, pinyon nuts, acorns, seeds of grass, yucca fruits, cactus fruits, wild gooseberries, wild grapes, and juniper berries. The fleshy leaves of the agave furnished a sweet nourishment. Numerous roots were also used for food. Thus, the natural environment supplied the Mogollon Indians with fibers for weaving textiles; with food; with narcotics, perhaps, from the Datura (jimson weed), specimens of which we have found in our early ruins; medicine; and probably vegetable dyes.

Thus I hope that it will be clear to the reader that there is a very direct relationship between geography, geology, climate and rainfall—environment, that is, mountains, canyons, river valleys, and deserts—and culture or civilization. Without all the plants mentioned in the last paragraph, the early dwellers in these areas would have had tough going. Nature, however, kindly provided a fair amount of rainfall, some permanent streams, narrow stream valleys or sometimes wider

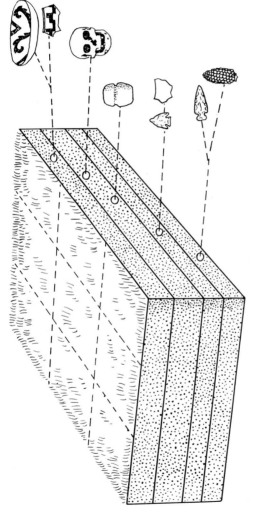

A CROSS SECTION OF DEBRIS IN A CAVE

An idealized sketch drawn to demonstrate stratigraphy (layering). By noting the layers and what is in them we can determine which layer is early and which is later. This is called relative chronology. Note that the axe is later than the plain potsherd and the ear of corn, but no absolute date can be assigned to any article. If the ear of corn is dated by Carbon 14 at 500 B.C. then we know that plain pottery came in after that time.

alluvial plains, a moderate climate that was not too cold or too hot, and an ample supply of wild game and natural products.

LANGUAGE AND CULTURE

Up to this point we have emphasized tools of stone and bone, typical remains, equipment of various kinds, houses, caves, and the like; but we haven't said much about symbols, patterns of conduct and organization of knowledge, and we usually take for granted man's greatest invention—language. Without it, no civilization would be possible.

It is now thought that language developed *before* man began to make or shape tools. It is conjectured that man must have developed a complex brain, symbols such as language and art, and a fair degree of insight at an earlier period than he developed tools. Unless man can talk he cannot think; and unless he thought about these things, it is probable that he could not have created inventions such as agriculture, or improved his breeds of plants, pottery, house-building, irrigation, and the like. This, then, is the big difference between man and the lower animals.

As has been pointed out by different writers, we must realize that although technical skills and social organization are important in man's development, the really "human" traits are language and thought and man's capacity for making use of his inventions—fire, tools, houses and the like—not only for his daily comfort and existence but for the creation of much greater things, such as art, religion, and necessary abstractions, and for the creation of individuals who stand out from the mass. One of man's greatest concerns, probably from time immemorial, has been with life after death, religion, the control of the supernatural—the control of forces greater than himself. We cannot understand the great pyramids of Mexico, the irrigation works of the ancient Hohokam Indians in southern Arizona, or the long, exhausting rituals of the Pueblo Indians without realizing that some of the greatest efforts of man have been used for expressing his feelings toward life and death. One might think that man would have spent his greatest efforts in creating better baskets and

Miscellaneous fragments of pottery. *Left row:* Development of design called "lines and solids" from early red on buff ware (top, A.D. 700) to late black on white ware (bottom, A.D. 1000). *Right row:* Development of design called "opposed saw-tooth lines" to "negative lightning" (top, A.D. 700; bottom, A.D. 1000).

pots, but that does not seem to have been the case. Certainly, his attitude was more spiritual and probably more realistic than our own present philosophy. I spoke earlier of the fact that sometimes archaeologists do not concentrate enough on patterns of conduct, organization of knowledge and social patterns of ancient peoples; and you may think that it is impossible to learn anything about these abstractions because they seem to have vanished as completely as perishable materials such as sandals and baskets. But I shall have some conjectures to make, even about these abstract subjects, later on in this book.

But let us return for the moment to more concrete matters and to our own excavations in New Mexico. What did we *know* about the Mogollon Indians and what did we *think* of them prior to our excavations? We knew practically nothing about them. Their existence had been pointed out by an archaeologist some five years before we started our work; but aside from his two excellent reports we had very little to go on.

CAUSES OF CULTURE CHANGE

We did have some general theories on which we felt we could depend and one of them is concerned with the ways in which cultures probably change. A brief statement may be of use. Cultures change, among other ways, by addition or loss of traits or—perhaps better stated—by replacement of traits. For example, the bow and arrow eventually replaced the spear thrower.

Replacements come about by (1) internal changes in the culture, that is, by "drift"; and (2) by contact and subsequent borrowing. Further reference to "drift" will be found in the last chapter, but here I may say that the term is taken over from a concept in linguistics. In language one can find a changing pattern that is brought about by invisible, impersonal, non-conscious influences. Drift is part of the life of language, a force that keeps it vital. In brief, language varies in time and space.

We have reason to believe that customs, artifacts, and architecture also change according to a non-conscious pattern.

Even cultures that are locked up in pockets of mountains and thus are remote and fairly isolated from contact with other cultures change, albeit more slowly. But change they do and according to a fairly well-established pattern. Thus without outside stimuli and contacts with other cultures, drift will occur.

The second mode of acquiring new traits that may replace well-established ones is by means of stimulations from the outside, by borrowing, by trade, and by wars.

In our own area we know that certain elements of culture, or traits, existed at or about 3500 B.C. and that later other changes could be recognized. After much digging and thinking we found out that a series of minor changes often added up to something that was major and that would be discernible in our records. Day-by-day changes, or even year-by-year alterations in the lives of these ancient people would hardly be discernible or recognizable in the dirt that we were throwing out of the pit-houses and caves. But when, as we dug from one level to another in a cave, we found that the people had had a certain kind of implement called the spear-thrower and that gradually it had been displaced by a bow and arrow, and that there had been other changes such as differences in styles of sandals, we had what might be called stimulations from outside. We feel thoroughly sure that none of these things were invented in our Pine Lawn area—that they were brought in from the outside by trade, by contact, or by some other means. Simply put, this means that we found definite changes in the levels of our caves or in early houses when we compared them with late ones; but we assumed that these were the results of gradual accumulations or cumulative episodes that finally mounted up into a major change of some kind or another. Certainly, when the people took up agriculture and depended less on gathering wild foods, roots and nuts, and less on hunting, there was a definite "culture change." It seems fairly obvious that when agriculture was introduced and accepted, other changes must have taken place in the culture at about the same time. What would such changes have been? First, probably, permanent villages would now have been possible and would have come into being, and, in fact, did so; second, the peoples living in certain areas and growing crops would have felt vested rights—property rights—in certain fertile, well-watered lands; and, third, some leisure time would have been available. With the creation of more leisure, life would have become easier and it would have been possible now for certain people to spend time on pursuits other than hunting for food; and thus we have the atmosphere ready for the advent of inventors, for inventions cannot be created without leisure time.

AGRICULTURE AND THE DIGGING STICK

We can hail the introduction of agriculture into the Mogollon area as a great step forward because the domestication and use of "tamed" plants is one of man's most important contributions and inventions. A great deal of cunning and devotion went into domestication of plants, and perhaps the cultivation of primitive domesticated corn was successful among the Mogollon Indians because they possessed an understanding of the biological processes of the wild plants that grew in the area and had unwittingly made many observations concerning them; and perhaps they even knew a little bit about hybridization. This, it seems to me, is as important a discovery as the digging stick, but archaeologists tend, in describing ancient cultures, to stress the digging stick and not think much of its meaning. What stands back of a digging stick? Centuries and centuries of observation and patient nurturing of plants so that finally a plant such as maize or corn (that comes from South America or Mexico) could be domesticated.

You may well ask at this point, "What is the purpose of archaeological work and of all this sweat and digging?" Farther on in this book I shall devote a chapter to the goals and aims of archaeology; but here let me briefly say that we hope by studying the ancient civilizations that now are dead that we may contribute to studies which will throw light on contemporary and future events in our own civilization. It may well be that if we can learn enough about man's past and his development we may make more vital advances and discoveries tomorrow than any that have yet been achieved.

Divisions of Mogollon

CULTURE and CHRONOLOGY

Now I should like to tell you bit by bit and era by era, something of the Mogollon civilization as it grew from very lowly and primitive beginnings and moved on to other areas.

The Mogollon Culture has been arbitrarily divided into a number of *phases* or *periods*.

Each phase or period of time indicates a more or less stable continuum and an *assemblage* (collection or group) of traits that remained comparatively the same from the beginning to the end of the phase. For example, one might find in the *X Phase* the following cluster of characteristics or traits: (1) projectile points for spears; (2) tools for grinding nuts and berries into a paste; (3) choppers or axes of stone that were not hafted (handled) but were held in the hand—thus called *hand-choppers;* (4) scrapers of stone for dressing hides; (5) hearths, square or round; and (6) mortars and pestles. Note that there is no mention of pottery, houses, or agriculture in this list of traits. One would expect to find most or

47

MOGOLLON COUNTRY NEAR PINE LAWN, NEW MEXICO

all of these traits in the *X Phase* wherever one encounters a site of this phase within a limited area.

When one digs a site that contains those six items plus the presence of pottery and pit-houses, then one arbitrarily creates another phase—the *Y Phase*, for example.

This arbitrary device of creating periods certainly corresponds to nothing the Indians would have recognized, but it does help the archaeologist to mark off changes and advances. The names that are chosen for the phases are usually taken from some local feature—the name of a ranch, a nearby mountain peak, a river, or a modern town.

Changes or innovations such as pottery-making or farming were probably adopted slowly, with no thought of the effects the changes would have on the future of the individuals in the group. In our own day, we have seen that automobiles have replaced the horse and buggy, but I feel certain that our immediate predecessors had no idea of the profound effects that autos have produced fifty years later.

Hence we might speak of the *horse and buggy*, the *automobile*, and the *atomic energy phases*. Such historical divisions as these are arbitrary, but they are meaningful in that they help us to differentiate one time in our history from another. They

Animal pendant of stone
(about A.D. 200).

Storage basket woven of yucca leaves on foundations of bundles of grass;
found in earliest layers of Tularosa Cave (about 300 B.C.).

49

help us classify and interpret great masses of unrelated facts.

A *phase*, then, represents a stage in the development of culture that occurs in a particular area at a specific period of time.

To put the matter in another way, we might think of the Cochise-Mogollon development as a long straight line that represents a continuous history of about 4,000 years in length. This line (or history) has been chopped up into a number of segments that are determined by significant changes in the assemblage of traits. Some are about a thousand years long and some only one or two hundred years long. Each segment, for convenience in classification, has been named.

The names of the various Cochise-Mogollon phases or periods along with their approximate dates are given below.

Sulphur Springs Period (a Cochise manifestation not yet found in Pine Lawn Valley, New Mexico), about 5000 to 2500 B.C.

Chiricahua Period (a Cochise complex that we did find in Pine Lawn Valley), about 2500 to 300 B.C.

Pine Lawn Period, 300 B.C. to A.D. 500.

Georgetown Period, A.D. 500 to 700.

San Francisco Period, A.D. 700 to 900.

Three Circle Period, A.D. 900 to 1000.

Reserve Period, A.D. 1000 to 1100.

Tularosa Period, A.D. 1100 to 1200.

Foote Canyon Period, A.D. 1200 to 1350.

I shall not refer to these periods very often, nor shall I describe the cultural assemblage of traits for each one! In treating the growth and development of the culture of the Mogollon Indians, I shall lump together the details of two or three periods and make note only of major changes in the culture.

To convert our archaeological information into culture history, we must have a time perspective—a viewpoint that will enable us to state which ruin or site is the oldest and which the youngest. We may develop a chronology that is only *relative*—a time reckoning that tells us the age of a particular site in relation to others; or we may, if fortunate, be able to establish an *absolute* chronology that will give us a date in terms of our calendar.

It might be of interest, however, to state briefly how the actual dates were assigned to the above periods.

There are several methods that are used for obtaining these dates in the Southwest; and sometimes, with luck, one or more methods may be combined.

One method of establishing relative chronology is by means of stratigraphy, which is the study of the position and

Bracelets made from shell imported by trade from Gulf of California. *Left one*, about A.D. 200; *right one*, about A.D. 1200.

order of the archaeological layers—rubbish, remains of buildings, or layers of occupation (p. 41). Generally speaking, we may say the oldest remains are at the bottom of the debris, and the youngest, the latest, on the top. If the remains of cultures of different sorts are found in each of four separate layers, it is then possible to establish a *relative* chronology for the four cultures.

When we can establish a chronological correlation of several ancient villages or camp sites or of two or more stratigraphic sequences in a restricted area we speak of this as *cross-dating*. *Cross-dating* is accomplished by comparing types of similar or nearly identical objects. To illustrate cross-dating I may cite two examples: (1) If we find projectile points and fragments of pottery of the same type in sites A and B we assume that the two sites are contemporaneous because we think that peoples of a restricted area would probably share a number of distinctive traits. Even in our own culture today a small town in Illinois is not very different from its counterpart in Arizona. (2) We get more satisfactory cross-dating if we find tools or ornaments from a dated site in an undated site. Such objects are called *trade pieces* because we assume that they reached the undated site as a result of trade.

Very ancient sites are sometimes dated by means of their association with old lake beaches or alluvial deposits formed during or shortly after the last glacial period; but climatic changes yield only approximate dates and are obtained only with the aid of competent geologists, paleontologists, and paleobotanists.

Perhaps one of the most amazing methods of obtaining an exact date for many of the ruins of the Southwest is by the use of tree rings. This means of dating is called *dendrochronology*. For details on this subject the reader is referred to the Bibliography (Douglass, 1929). Briefly, tree-ring dating may be defined as a system of establishing an absolute chronology by counting the rings found in the logs of trees, especially those of pine, Douglas fir, and pinyon. The system is based on the fact that trees are responsive to seasonal changes, to rainfall, and to drought. In years of considerable rainfall the rings are wide; in dry years they are narrow. In counting and studying the rings, one finds certain patterns of wet and dry years (wide and narrow rings) which are not usually duplicated. One counts the rings and notes the sequence thereof in an old living pine tree perhaps 500 years old. Then if we find another log (from the roof of an early Spanish mission or an early historic pueblo) we can correlate the outer rings of this roof beam with the inner rings of the living pine tree. Cross-dating is carried on from log to log until early prehistoric times have been reached. A graph of the pattern of wet and dry years is then made up. It is based on many tree records in order to exclude errors. This is used for rendering the year in which the roof beams of a particular village were cut. At present the tree-ring calendar extends back to about 59 B.C.

An absolute chronology can also be established by using the *radiocarbon* method of dating, which determines the age of organic archaeological materials by measuring the amount of carbon 14 they contain. All living matter contains radioactive carbon (carbon 14). When a plant or an animal dies, it ceases to absorb carbon 14, but the radioactive element gradually decays at a constant and known rate. The number of years that have elapsed since the death of the organism is determined by measuring the degree to which the carbon 14 has decayed. At the present time, our limit of determination of ancient specimens made of wood, bone, fibers, leather, or other parts of animals or plants is about 40,000 years.

All of these methods have been used to establish Mogollon chronology. Some of the dates are estimated and some are fairly exact, but even the latter may be in error by a hundred years or more. Even so, these dates are exact enough for our purposes. Certainly, fifty years ago, such computation would have been impossible because the various scientific tools had not been created.

SOURCE OF SOME MOGOLLON TRAITS

Recent information concerning agriculture and pottery, especially, and perhaps concerning other traits too, leads us to believe that many Mogollon characteristics came from Mexico. We shall be more certain of the verity of these assumptions in a few years. At present, we can only state that the various Southwestern civilizations referred to in an earlier chapter—the Hohokam, the Anasazi, the Patayan, and the Mogollon—were all interrelated.

Twenty-five years ago, we were impressed mostly with the differences between the four cultures. Now, as a result of digging, comparing, studying, arguing, and dating, we can see the relationship. For example, as the result of a recent research project at this Museum covering over 6,000 pottery fragments and hundreds of whole pots, we can make fairly definite statements about the designs on painted pottery in the Southwest from about A.D. 500 to 1300. Although types of pottery from various areas—Snaketown in southern Arizona, Mesa Verde in southwestern Colorado, Chaco Canyon in north central New Mexico, Flagstaff in Arizona, and the Pine Lawn-Reserve area in west central New Mexico—can easily be differentiated, similar designs occur in these areas at about the same times and serve to tie the areas together developmentally. One finds on early painted pottery throughout the Southwest in the same century, an abundance of simple geometric designs of lines and solid figures; in later times, in the same century, the pottery shows a progression to more complicated designs with hatched and solid figures and combinations of many elements.

Pottery designs showing such synchronous or simultaneous changes throughout the Southwest are sometimes called "horizon styles." This term implies the frequent use of a distinctive design element such as simple geometric designs of broad lines or the use of realistic portrayals of animals or human figures at a given time period (for example, from A.D. 700 to 900) throughout the Southwest. "Horizon" in this sense, then, refers to a specific time period and to a wide horizon or area. Thus, horizon styles help to interrelate regions and to link together several cultures. The cultures may be and often are diverse, but the same specific and distinctive designs on the pots throughout the area may be the result of diffusion and trade, the spread of a religious cult, or the actual intermixture of peoples.

Out of the study that produced the knowledge of horizon styles in the Southwest, and other related researches, we have evolved another abstract idea that we call the "co-tradition" of the Southwest. This unwieldy term simply means that the various civilizations and traditions of the Southwest have parallel and allied developments and that all of them underwent rather uniform growth and ultimately reached a similar stage of development. That is to say that all of the Southwestern cultures at one time built pit-houses, practiced agriculture, made distinctive pottery, and shared many other religious and everyday features; but it does not imply that all of them possessed the total assemblage of Southwestern traits. The Hohokam Indians, for example, lived in pit-houses, but, so far as we now know, did not ever live in cellular or multi-roomed apartment houses on top of the ground as did the Anasazi and the Mogollon Indians.

What the co-tradition really means is that the Southwest should be considered as a whole, a cultural sphere, composed of many related parts. Each civilization within its borders is not a unique expression of culture, but each is related to the others in a greater or less degree.

A LONG UNBROKEN HISTORY

Before closing this chapter, I shall describe briefly the relationship of the Mogollon and other Southwestern cultures to the greater Southwest or Desert cultures and touch briefly on possible linguistic affiliations and time perspectives.

According to the most recent studies, the ancestors of the founders of the Hohokam, Mogollon, Anasazi, and Patayan civilizations shared a culture or a way of life with many other Indians inhabiting the Intermontane area between the Rockies and the Sierra Nevada mountain ranges. This territory includes parts or all of the states of Washington, Oregon, Montana, Idaho, California, Nevada, Utah, Colorado, Wyoming, Arizona, and New Mexico, and western Texas and much of northern Mexico. This great Desert Culture area was probably one of the first to be inhabited by man, as the Carbon 14 dates for some sites take us back at least to 10,000 B.C. Many of the Cochise and early Mogollon traits are similar to if not identical with corresponding items in the Desert Culture of Utah, Oregon, Wyoming, and the other desert states. Thus, the local specializations of Cochise-Mogollon, Hohokam, and Anasazi arose from this unique and basic Desert Culture.

It is interesting to note that this geographical area was inhabited not only by a people (perhaps all related) who

55

shared a common culture, but in early historic times (Spanish conquest, about A.D. 1600) was likewise the homeland of a people who spoke from ten to twenty different dialects, all of which are related and grouped under the heading of Uto-Aztekan linguistic stock.

We may say then that most of the Intermontane area lying between the Sierra Nevada and Rocky Mountains was inhabited (at about A.D. 1600) by Uto-Aztekan–speaking peoples.

I shall abridge the ideas set forth in a recent hypothesis concerning the relationship of archaeology, ethnology, linguistics, and physical anthropology of the Uto-Aztekan peoples who were spread over the west from Idaho to Mexico City. A few reasonable assumptions were made in this study. One was that physical type, language, and general culture patterns are generally more stable and enduring than are material objects such as pottery or houses, for example. Another was that the Intermontane area has been occupied by the Uto-Aztekan–speaking peoples for at least 3000 years and perhaps much longer. If the Intermontane area was not completely peopled by Uto-Aztekan peoples, we can guess with more certainty that a nucleus of them was concentrated in the upper Gila and upper Little Colorado rivers in New Mexico and Arizona. This last guess is backed up by a preliminary study of comparative linguistics, and from this a dating has been arrived at by the study of the changes in basic vocabulary (see in Bibliography, *Dating by Words*, by Martin, for explanation of how this is done). The locale was established by the fact that certain words, such as "pine tree" and "juniper tree," indicate an intermediate altitude zone such as might be found in mountainous areas of the upper Gila River drainage.

Thus, we see how the weight of careful research can bear on particular problems and how some answers can be tentatively reached or guessed at.

Rope Snares. *Upper corner:* a bundle of six just as found. *Remainder:* snares from a second bundle, opened to show size and workmanship. From earliest level in Tularosa Cave (about 300 B.C. or earlier).

The TIME of

Limited WANDERING

About 6000 B.C. TO 500 B.C.

This section will describe various aspects of the daily life of the Mogollon Indians from the earliest times to A.D. 1350, at which time they abandoned forever a most attractive area.

In presenting my tale, I shall draw on materials from the excavations that we have made and on modern counterparts or similarities in the cultures of present-day Southwestern Indians.   I shall also present some guesses, hypotheses, or interpretations based on these data and I shall label them as conjectures or shall qualify their status by the use of such adverbs as probably, likely, and presumably.

I shall gather together several millennia or centuries in my descriptions and treat such *parcels* as units without going into a mass of detail for every historical period that has been set up.   These *parcels* or groupings are chosen partly for convenience and partly because each contains significant innovations or shifts in the cultural pattern.

MAKING A LIVING

The problem of obtaining food confronted the early Co-chise–Mogollon Indians as it always has and always will confront all peoples.

These Indians solved the problem more or less successfully in a number of ways, but, so far as we can now tell, with little or no aid from the practice of agriculture. The idea of planting and tending certain favorite seed-yielding plants was probably not novel to them. Corn, the plant that later became so important in their lives, was probably introduced to the Mogollon Indians between 4000 and 2000 B.C. At first, it may have been regarded as a mere addition to their diet of seeds. Apparently, it took some time for them to recognize the great merit of corn-growing.

In the main, then, we regard this era as one in which collecting wild edible foods was the principal way of making a living, although the Indians also did some hunting. The foods most commonly eaten were pinyon nuts, walnuts, acorns, grass seeds, gourds, yucca fruits, cactus, gooseberries, and agave.

The population was probably not sedentary, but moved about in a fairly restricted area from one gathering ground to another, intensively exploiting the environment as thoroughly as possible. Reliance was not placed on a crop or on any single resource but was put rather on adapting their appetites to all the local plants, insects, small mammals, and birds. The seeds harvested were ground into flour and were cooked as mush or were parched. Products of other plants were either eaten raw or were boiled in baskets (no pottery); game may have been roasted. There was probably no big-game hunting.

TOOLS

The tool inventory for this period (6000 to 500 B.C.) is fairly extensive for a non-sedentary folk and consisted of flat or basin-type milling-grinding stones; pestles; knives and choppers made by the percussion method that produced large flakes, cores, and spalls; the tumpline for carrying burdens;

Earliest ceremonial room (Great Kiva) in Reserve–Pine Lawn area; fire hearth and storage pits in center; purpose of groove in floor not known (about 300 B.C. to A.D. 200).

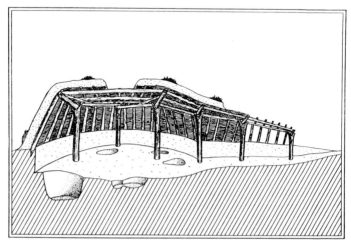

Cross section of Mogollon pit-house shown on opposite page.

Early Mogollon pit-house in process of excavation. Burial in left floor-pit; storage floor-pits in foreground; tunnel entrance at top (about 300 B.C. to A.D. 200).

the atlatl or throwing stick (no bow and arrow); snares; small projectile points; the digging stick (used down to the present time); baskets, mostly twined, used in gathering, storing, and boiling foods; nets; wooden bunts and pointed hardwood sticks thrown from the spear-throwers; and flat, curved wooden clubs. The dog (present by 4000 B.C.) was possibly used in the chase and for food.

This brief inventory of food-gathering tools, coupled with our knowledge of the ways in which the Paiutes and other desert dwellers eked out an existence in Utah and Nevada in the 1850's, enables us to guess that these early Cochise-Mogollon people had made an excellent adaptation to their environment.

Thus, we can see in retrospect that the habits of food-gathering and the ways of preparing the food—flour-cookery, parching, boiling, and roasting—and all the customs that this emphasis entails, would have made it easy for the Cochise-Mogollon people to pass from a food-gathering stage to farming. If these Indians had been big-game hunters, it would have been more difficult for us to envision a transition from dependence on hunting to dependence on agriculture.

PREPARATION OF FOODS

As noted above, foods were broiled, boiled in baskets (no pottery), roasted, or baked in ashes; seeds were placed in shallow baskets and parched with live coals. Cooking must have been done in the open as we know of no houses for this period. Judging by the number of milling stones found at early sites, the favorite way of preparing food was to grind seeds and perhaps nuts to flour and then cook them as mush. Some flour made from wild seeds may have been made up into patties or cakes and packed in holes in the ground for future use. Some flour-mush batter may have been baked on slabs of stone or on the ground by raking coals and ashes over it. Grinding was done on milling stones or with mortars and pestles. Deer and small mammals were roasted or barbecued in pits by placing hot stones below and above the meat. Seasoning was probably haphazard, as salt in even a relatively impure form was not abundant and perhaps was only obtained by trade. Alkaline or saline earth and water were acceptable substitutes, since all animals and men must ingest some salt daily. The

Mentzelia (blazing star) seeds stored in plain-ware pottery jar in Cordova Cave, New Mexico (about A.D. 200). Seeds were parched, ground and eaten.

milling stones (metates) were cleaned and scoured with wads of plant fibers from yucca, agave, grasses, and woody stems. Fires, especially in caves, were probably carefully tended and nursed so that they would not go out; but, when they did, a fire drill and hearth (much like the type the Boy Scouts use today) were available for creating new fire.

I have referred to "boiling in baskets" and this statement may be mystifying; but cooking in baskets is not difficult. If a basket is woven very well and tightly, it will hold liquids. If the weaving is somewhat coarse, the basket may be made water-tight by painting pitch on the inner or outer surfaces. In such a water-tight container, the Indians would place the food to be boiled. Hot stones would then be added to the food

Earliest undecorated Mogollon pottery from pit-houses
(about 300 B.C. to A.D. 200).

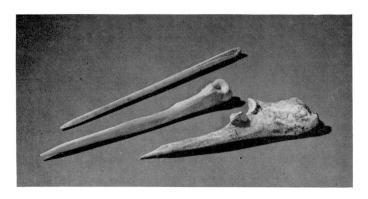

Bone awls.   Upper two, about A.D. 100; lower one, about A.D. 1200.

basket. This manner of cooking food is sometimes known as "stone boiling." If the boiling subsided and the food was not done, the cool stones would be removed and hot ones substituted.

UTILIZATION AND PROCESSING OF RAW MATERIALS

Tools were manufactured principally from stone, wood, and bone. The preferred kinds of stone were basalt, andesite, and quartzite, all tough materials. From these were made hand choppers, hammerstones, and rubbing and abrading stones. There were no hafted axes at this time. Projectile points, blades, knives, scrapers and other pressure-chipped implements were produced from flint, chalcedony, and obsidian. Milling stones (metates) and manos and mortars and pestles were made from igneous rocks such as rhyolite and trachyte. Various woods, such as oak, pine, willow, and mountain mahogany, were utilized for making spear-throwers, darts or spears, bunts, digging sticks, fire drills and hearths, "trowels," scoops, ladles, awls, and weaving tools. Bows and arrows were not known to these people at this time.

Awls, flakers, fleshers, wrenches and beads came from the bones of deer and antelope.

Basketry is the sole container that has been preserved for us from the period before the advent of pottery. If boxes or bark buckets were known to these Indians, none have survived. It seems safe to assume that basketry was an important item in the household. A basket, if smeared with pitch, would have served as a water container; if it had been partly filled with water, red-hot stones and meat or ground-up seeds, it would have served as a cooking vessel (a fireless cooker). Baskets could also have been used for storing foods, for gathering seeds, nuts, and berries, and for transporting loads. The materials for basket-making consisted of woody shoots, grasses, yucca leaves, and sotol.

Blankets were made of rabbit fur cut up into strips and woven together by twining. Wickerwork sandals were woven from yucca leaves, and string aprons and sashes were made from vegetable fibers or animal hair. We do not know that

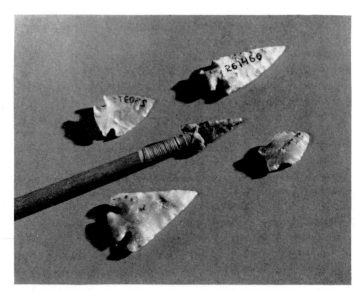

Projectile points. Two at *left* date from about A.D. 1000; two at *right*, 100 B.C. In center is modern hafted projectile point to illustrate method probably used by Mogollon Indians to haft their points.

Choppers and tobacco pipe of stone. *Left*, chopper (about A.D. 1000); *right*, chopper (about 300 B.C.); pipe, about A.D. 200.

TULAROSA CAVE (MIDDLE FOREGROUND), NEW MEXICO
Photograph taken from across canyon

cloth was woven at this time. Cradles or "nests" were made from sotol leaves; matting, from yucca rushes; burden straps, or tumplines, from bear grass and cords of hard vegetable fibers. Cordage, carrying nets, and snares for catching small mammals were spun and woven from vegetable fibers of yucca or other plants. Shell bracelets were made from shells obtained from the Gulf of California, probably by trade.

This brief summary will indicate how well adapted the people were to their environment and how well they used almost every plant for particular needs, and how well the animal bones and available rocks were used for making tools of all sorts.

DIVISION OF LABOR

On the basis of our knowledge of modern Indians, we assume that the women gathered the wild foods and plants, fetched the water, prepared and cooked the meals, served the food and did the sewing. The food was served in large wild gourds split in half, or in baskets. The sewing was done with sinew thread and bone needles.

The men hunted and set the snares, wove baskets, scraped and prepared skins for clothing, and manufactured all tools and ornaments.

HOUSES AND HOME LIFE

Actually very little can be said about this subject. Present evidence indicates that houses were unknown during this period or at least during the earliest part of it.

Caves, rock shelters, and overhangs were probably the favorite locations for settlements. In these, along with the tools and household goods, have been found bark or grass beds.

It is barely possible that skin shelters or tents were known and used. It is also possible that crude windbreaks of twigs and boughs were utilized for very cool or rainy weather, but the perishable nature of such constructions precludes our finding them now. Thus, evidence on this point may never be found.

68

We suspect that the social organization of these people was similar to that of present day food-gathering tribes, in which inheritance and descent are through both the father-line and the mother-line. The mother, father and children of these ancient people lived together and probably constituted a unit that we call a nuclear family.

PREPARATIONS FOR RELIGIOUS CEREMONIES

Little can be said with certainty on this subject. We guess that these Indians held some sort of religious beliefs, but proof is lacking. Evidence for our guess comes from a few objects that appear to have had no practical reason for existence and resemble ceremonial objects of later stages.

These objects are incised sticks; prayer-sticks used perhaps for wafting prayers heavenward to the gods; pieces of raw mineral paint such as ochres; stones or palettes on which the paint was ground to fine powder for possible use as body paint; crystals possibly used in curing illness; and small toothpick-like sticks on which were impaled juniper berries (called juniper-berry skewers). We have no idea what part in religious or healing ceremonies these skewers played, but they served no practical purpose that *we* can think of. They have been found in cultural debris that dates as late as A.D. 900.

From an examination of the life and customs of the Ute and Paiute Indians, who were formerly food-gatherers and whose culture is assumed to have resembled that of the early Cochise-Mogollon Indians, we can make one or two suppositions concerning the ancient religion. It is assumed that the Cochise-Mogollon Indians held certain religious beliefs in which the relationship between human beings and supernatural powers was largely a matter of individual concern. Every person may have hoped to acquire a guardian spirit who would assist him in hunting and in maintaining health. Shamans or medicine men may have existed and their duties would have been to heal the sick or wounded. Minor collective or group ceremonies may have existed to help the tribe in promoting general fertility and in finding foods. We do not know whether they believed in a life in the hereafter.

EMERGENCE of Small, Sedentary

COMMUNITIES

ABOUT 500 B.C. TO A.D. 1000

The periods covered in this chapter (500 B.C. to A.D. 1000) include part of the Chiricahua period and all of the Pine Lawn, Georgetown, San Francisco and Three Circle periods (see p. 50). Information concerning this span of 1500 years is somewhat fuller than that for the preceding period, because of increasing population more intensive archaeological investigation, and more abundant artifacts and better preservation of them. We may, then, describe the life and activities of this span with considerably more certainty. Furthermore, we shall witness the beginnings of village life and the development of certain traditions that lasted many centuries.

MAKING A LIVING

In the last chapter, I suggested that in earliest times the Mogollon Indians subsisted principally on wild edible plants.

Certainly they did some hunting, also. It is likewise probable that by 2000 B.C. at least, maize was present in the Mogollon area, but, as stated earlier, the basic Cochise-Mogollon pattern was not much modified by the presence of this plant. It would seem that the people regarded corn merely as an addition to the wild plants that were gathered and eaten.

But in this period (500 B.C. to A.D. 1000) we find an increasing appreciation and use of corn as well as squash and beans, both of which had put in an appearance by 1000 B.C. The greater dependence on agriculture must have been due in part to a realization that here was an excellent safeguard against starvation, provided the group as a whole moved toward the goal of more farming and less gathering, and provided the surplus could be safely stored and protected from weather, rodents, enemies, and shiftless relatives.

Judging from our excavations in Tularosa and Cordova Caves, some game was also taken and eaten and many wild plants and seeds were still collected to supplement, enrich, and vary the diet. But by 500 to 200 B.C. agriculture was really flourishing and was by then the primary means of subsistence for the Mogollon Indians.

We do not know exactly where corn originated. Recent researches suggest, however, that the wild ancestor of corn grew in favorable spots in the Amazonian jungles of South America. From there, corn spread northward through Mexico (where new types may have arisen) to North America, reaching the Mogollon Indians in the form of a tropical flint corn by 2000 B.C. or earlier.

Rudimentary farming knowledge and primitive farming tools and techniques were already possessed by the Cochise people, who shared the Desert Culture traits with all the other Indians from Oregon to Mexico City and from the Rocky Mountains to the Pacific Coast. Also present by 5000 to 2000 B.C. were digging sticks (almost exactly the same as Southwestern Indian farmers use today), baskets used for collecting and storing food, milling stones for reducing seeds to flour, and a long tradition of parching seeds, cooking flour-and-mush and preparing and cooking seed plants.

71

MUSEUM DIORAMA DISPLAYING PROBABLE APPEARANCE OF A PIT–HOUSE VILLAGE
IN THE YEAR 200 B.C.

Pit-house in left background is same as one shown on page 61

The artist's reconstruction is based entirely on information procured by the work of archaeological expeditions sent by Chicago Natural History Museum to western New Mexico.

A pit-house was an excavated area, several feet in depth and 12 to 15 feet in diameter; which, when roofed, made a snug dwelling. The hard-packed unexcavated dirt served as basal portions of the walls. The roof, supported by one or more upright posts, consisted of large and small poles, branches, and a thick covering of sod or hard-packed adobe (mud). The floors were smooth, hard-packed dirt. The entrance was a low passage opening to the east.

The origin of the Mogollon pit-houses is not known. It is probable that such houses have a long history, and possible connections with similar structures in portions of eastern Asia, the Ukraine, and Czechoslovakia.

73

Therefore, it is no surprise that corn and, later, beans and squash were readily adopted by these people, who, in a sense, were predestined to become farmers and whose lives were bound to have a memorable effect on 150 later generations of Southwestern Indians.

HYBRIDIZATION OF CORN

During this era of 1500 years (500 B.C. to A.D. 1000) the races and strains of maize were improved by hybridization with corn brought from other areas, and the number of ker-

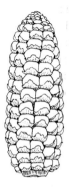

Early ear of corn (pod corn) of the type grown about 1000 B.C. Reconstruction based on ear excavated at Tularosa Cave, New Mexico; drawing by Gustav Dalstrom, assisted by Dr. Hugh C. Cutler. Length about 1½ inches.

nel-rows dropped from 16 to 14, 12, and 8. This meant more "efficient" corn, as each kernel was bigger and juicier and contained more nourishment. The introduced varieties were vigorous types; hence, there was an advantage in growing the hardier varieties and in cross-fertilizing the older local varieties with new races.

Surplus supplies of corn, beans, and squash may have occurred as time went on, and these may have been distributed to friends and relatives in order that prestige and dignity might accrue from such generous acts. Certainly with a more dependable food supply there would have been leisure and with it more progress in all ways of life.

USE OF GAME FOR FOOD

As I indicated above, hunting was never a very significant item in Mogollon life, but it must be remembered that smaller game was probably always hunted to a certain extent. Evidence for this statement comes from the bones of deer, turkeys, dogs, pocket gophers, squirrels, coyotes, mountain sheep, lynx, sage hens, rabbits, wolves, antelopes, and badgers, found in the village middens, on house floors, and in cave refuse. The most frequently hunted animal was apparently the white-tailed deer.

Animals were bagged in various ways. Early in the period spears and spear throwers (atlatls), snares, nets, and traps were used. About or after the beginning of the Christian era, bows and arrows were introduced and gradually replaced the atlatl and the snares. By A.D. 900 the atlatl and the snares had completely disappeared from the Mogollon inventory. Nets, used especially on rabbit drives, were still employed. Crops were planted and wild foods dug up by means of a wooden digging stick (still used); and harvested crops and wild foods were transported in large baskets by means of tumplines. Corn was planted in hills, with squash and beans interspersed.

PREPARATION OF FOODS

Methods of cooking probably did not change much. Meats were broiled or stewed; corn and possibly other vegetables were roasted, parched or baked in ashes or pits; seeds were parched with live coals in shallow baskets; and corn was popped on the cob. These were perhaps the chief methods of cooking. Corn, beans, and squashes were frequently boiled or roasted and combined in succotash. Hominy may also have been prepared and eaten. Corn was reduced to flour on metates with manos, the upper grinding stone, and some foods were crushed up in mortars with pestles. Manos, metates, and perhaps cooking pots were cleaned and scoured with yucca pods. Foods to be held over were stored in sealed pits in the house floors, in sealed caches in caves, in pottery jars, and perhaps in baskets.

Pottery was introduced into the Pine Lawn area by 300 B.C. and perhaps earlier. It gradually replaced baskets as cooking

Bag of bison skin that had contained squash seeds shown in lower half of illustration (about A.D. 600)

and storage receptacles. Gourd vessels made convenient ladles and drinking cups.

The most common foods were maize, beans, squash, gourds, yucca pods, cacti, black walnuts, acorns, grass seeds, desert primrose leaves, and sunflower seeds.

Cooking was done, in the latter part of the era, more and more inside the houses.

UTILIZATION AND PROCESSING OF RAW MATERIALS

Visitors to our archaeological excavations frequently express surprise at the energy, diligence, and enterprise of the prehistoric Mogollon Indians and ask: "How did they make this?" "What tools did they have?" "Did they have metal tools?"

Our visitors are filled with wonderment when we tell them that the Mogollones had a fairly complete stock of tools at their disposal. But no metal tools were ever made or used by

76

these peoples, although small copper tinklers (probably imported from Mexico) have been found in some sites dated after A.D. 1100.

It may be safely said that almost every available natural resource was converted to man's needs and instrumentality. The chief raw materials used for tools, weapons, dress, textiles,

Tools of stone. *Left*, hammerstone (about A.D. 200); *right*, scraper (about A.D. 700)

amusement, and ceremonies were stone, plant fibers, wood, bone, shell, and clay.

Let us examine briefly some of the objects made from these materials.

STONE ARTIFACTS

Metates, manos and pestles were produced from volcanic stone; door- and baking-slabs from sandstone; hand choppers, hammerstones, grooved mauls, rubbing and abrading stones from tough rocks such as basalt, andesite, and quartzite; projectile and spear points, blades, knives, scrapers, drills, gravers and saws from flint; hoes from rhyolite; tobacco pipes from volcanic rocks; pigments from iron ores, limonite, magnetite and hematite; and divining stones from crystals.

There are no fewer than nineteen major tool types, all made of stone, and several sub-types.

USES OF PLANTS

From plants or plant fibers (not counting those of wood) there are nineteen classes of artifacts, with many subdivisions. I shall note some of the major and minor items, to exemplify the astonishing range: Sandals of several types of weaves; string aprons; sashes of twisted cord; snares; beds and cradles; netted carrying bags; strap and tumplines used to carry burdens; torches; brushes; needles of yucca spines; basketry of three different weaves; matting; cloth of bast or cotton fiber; cordage, bits of which were tied with seven different types of knots (square, granny, overhand, single half hitch, clove hitch, lark's head, and single bow); and netting. The more common plants for these articles were cotton, bast fibers, yucca, and rushes. Sometimes human and animal hair was spun, and tanned animal skins were fashioned into sandals and robes.

WOODEN TOOLS

Twenty-eight different types of artifacts were fashioned from wood. We have a fair guess as to the techniques used by the Mogollon Indians in woodworking. The techniques are recognizable from marks remaining on the specimens and from unfinished pieces. The woodworking methods seem to have included peeling the bark, breaking, whittling, splitting, drilling, sawing, scraping, incising, smoothing, and polishing. Tools used for fashioning artifacts were of stone, and they comprise choppers, scrapers, knives, drills, saws, files, and polishing stones.

The plants from which wooden artifacts were made include oak, pine, willow, mountain mahogany, juniper, reed, yucca, bear grass, and cliff rose. The artifacts made from these materials represent a wide range of interest, skill, and necessity. A glance at the following abbreviated inventory will confirm this statement: the atlatl or spear thrower; atlatl foreshafts and mainshafts; spears; bows and arrows; digging sticks; trowels; scoops; fire-drills and hearths; spoons and ladles; knife handles; awls; weaving tools; seed-beaters; torches; reed cigarettes that were filled with tobacco; carved prayer-sticks; dice; and reed flutes.

BONE TOOLS

Animal bones (mostly deer bones) were skillfully converted into awls of several types, punches, arrow-head flakers, weaving tools, beads, pennants and dice. It is probable that the larger bone tools such as awls and punches were made from animal longbones that were split by sawing a groove with a stone saw and then wedging the broken sections apart when the groove was deep enough. The ends could then be cut, ground, and polished to shape. Some tools were made from bone splinters while others were fashioned from a whole bone in such a way as to include the head of the bone as a handle.

ORNAMENTS

Bracelets, beads, and pendants were cut, sawed, or carved from a bivalve shell that was imported by trade from the Gulf of California.

USES OF CLAY

Local clays were extensively used for making pottery, and some other artifacts were also turned out: figurines, animal effigies, spindle whorls, clay balls (function unknown), and tobacco pipes.

ORIGIN OF MOGOLLON POTTERY

The origin of Mogollon pottery is an interesting problem to which there is no certain answer at present. Most archaeologists guess that the source may be Meso-American. Plain brown and polished red pottery in simple bowls and jars occurs in early Mexican cultures on the eastern slopes of the Sierra Madre Occidental Mountains from Chihuahua to Zacatecas. The earliest Mogollon ceramics are likewise plain brown and polished red wares in bowl and jar forms. But our assumption of a Mexican origin for Mogollon pottery is only the best one

Red on brown jar, the earliest type of painted pottery. Reconstructed from potsherds (about A.D. 700).

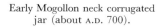

Early Mogollon neck corrugated jar (about A.D. 700).

that can be advanced at the present time. This idea is strengthened somewhat by the assumption that agriculture was probably derived from a Mexican source. If this be so, it may be that pottery itself and the methods for making it were also introduced and traded from a Meso-American source.

It should be remembered that the earliest Mogollon pottery (dating from 300 B.C.) is not crude or primitive. It is simple but far advanced beyond the experimental and incipient stages. It is well shaped and constructed by coiling, thinned by scraping, smoothed by means of a polishing stone, and

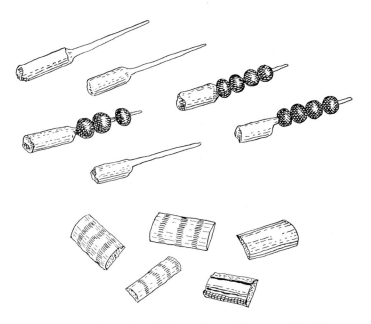

Ceremonial objects from Tularosa Cave. About A.D. 200–800.
Upper, juniper-berry skewers; *lower*, wooden dice.

well fired. No one at present, then, credits the Mogollon Indians with the invention of pottery. We all agree that it was a trait introduced from the south, as was agriculture.

The importance of pottery-making as an aid to housekeeping can hardly be exaggerated. Pottery vessels are useful for a variety of domestic purposes.

It is possible that creating pottery forms and then decorating some of the vessels served as a vent for the expression of aesthetic and religious feelings. From another point of view, the art of pottery-making may serve as a rough gauge of the progress a people has made on the road to "civilization."

At any rate, from any point of view, vessels of fired clay are convenient. Pottery, when present, is one of the most useful tools of the archaeologist for determining the relative age of a site. By comparing the form, decoration, or material of the pottery from many excavated sites, the archaeologist is able to work out the rise and fall in popularity of certain types. In other words, he studies the "fashions" of pottery types and is able to determine their sequence. This kind of comparison is invaluable in setting up a comparative chronology in a specific area.

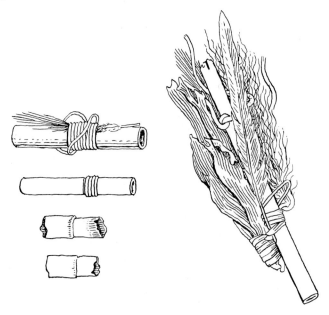

Cigarettes made of reeds filled with tobacco (earliest reported use of tobacco about A.D. 200–800).

HOW POTTERY WAS MADE

No living person has seen a Mogollon Indian make a pot; but because contemporary Southwestern Indian pottery superficially resembles Mogollon pottery, we assume that it may have been made in the same way. Carefully chosen clay that has been winnowed to remove twigs and gravel is mixed with a "temper" or "grog" (sand or crushed rocks) and is then wetted and kneaded. When ready for molding, the clay has the consistency of putty.

The potter's wheel was unknown to the Mogollones; therefore molding and shaping were done by hand by what is known as the *coil* method. This method makes use of long coils of clay. The potter forms the base of the future pot by pressing it out of a lump of properly tempered clay or by using the end of a roll of clay that has coiled on itself. The base thus formed is then placed in a shallow basket in which the growing vessel rests. The potter next builds up the walls of the pot by the addition of coils of clay which are either long enough to go around the walls more than once, producing a spiral effect, or are just long enough to go around once. This operation is repeated until the vessel has been completed.

If the coils are to be obliterated this task is done with a piece of gourd or a polishing stone. If the vessel is to be painted, this is done after the vessel has been dried in the air. Pigments were made from hematite (red) and magnetite (black). Designs, layouts, and color schemes require considerable sophistication, artistic ability, and skill. The Mogollon design and layouts are distinctive. They evolved over the centuries from simple broad-line patterns to involved arrangements of geometric forms such as squares, hatched diagonal lines, interlocking scrolls, and triangles.

"TYPES" OF POTTERY

The "cooking" pottery was usually a plain brown ware or unpainted type that is known as neck-banded, scored, or plain corrugated. These types are classed as *textured wares*. Banding and corrugations are merely the original coils that were not obliterated because it was the style to let them remain visible. *Scoring* was done with a blunt tool by which the surface was scratched.

EARLIEST POTTERY

The earliest Mogollon pottery was plain brown and plain red ware and lacked any painted designs or surface treatment. Cooking, storage, and serving of foods were all done in these types, which may be dated at about 300 B.C. or possibly earlier. These two types displayed a remarkable longevity, since they continued to be utilized right up to the time the

Mogollones moved out of the Pine Lawn Reserve area. In other words, these two major wares were made for more than 1,500 years.

NEW UTILITY AND PAINTED WARES

At approximately A.D. 400 to 600 several new types evolved: one that displayed neck-banding; another, scoring; another, "punched" surfaces; and, most important of all, a painted type with designs in red painted on a pink or brown background. With these new types the old favorites (plain brown and plain red wares) continued to be made and loved. In fact, as one can observe, after pottery appeared at about 300 B.C. no new types were formulated for almost 800 or 900 years! (The same conservatism may also be observed in architecture, in tools of stone, bone, and wood and in other traits in varying degrees.)

SMUDGED AND NEW PAINTED TYPES

Several centuries later, these types still persisted; and one finds, in addition, several variants of the textured wares and a "smudged" type. This type, later to become fairly popular, was usually confined to bowls, the insides of which are a polished black. The black was produced by permitting smoke or carbon to be deposited on the interiors, thus producing a *smudged* effect. The painted decorated pottery bore designs similar to those on the earlier pottery, but they now were done in red on a white background. A small bit of black on white painted pottery appeared toward the end of this period.

It should be noted that the earliest Mogollon wares and all the cooking types (whether banded, incised, punched, scored, or indented) are brown or red or brown-reds. Formerly, this predilection for browns and reds was assumed to be the result of a special firing technique supposedly used by the Mogollon Indians. This technique of firing is called the *oxidizing atmosphere*. We now feel that the brown and red colors of the pottery-paste and of the surface of unpainted wares were more likely produced by the clays that were available to the Mogol-

Red on white pottery bowl
(about A.D. 800).

Black on white pottery
bowl from an early town
(about A.D. 1000).

lon Indians. These clays were mostly volcanic or igneous in origin and the iron content tended to cause the pottery to become brown or red after it had been fired.

Briefly, Mogollon pottery in the incipient (300 B.C.) stages was uniformly unpainted brown or slipped (coated) red. The vessels were hand- or pebble-smoothed and manifest faintly irregular surfaces. They are simple in form. Later ceramics (A.D. 600–900) are marked by a continuation of earlier types, with the addition of smudged types, textured types (surface treatments such as scoring, incising, and corrugations or un-obliterated coils), and types bearing painted designs in red on backgrounds varying from brown through pink to white

85

and with designs that increasingly reflect refinements, innovations, and complexities. Continuity and change are observable in this period of pottery-making (300 B.C. to A.D. 1000), and it is probable that Mogollon potters directly or indirectly influenced the potters of other, nearby areas.

The earliest shapes were bowls or jars. Later, other shapes, such as ladles and pitchers, were developed.

HOUSES

In the preceding chapter I described a way of life that involved a certain amount of wandering about in search of food. This type of existence effectively prevented the establishment of villages and a sedentary life.

However, some time before 1000 B.C. several important innovations were introduced into the area and these radically changed the existence of the Cochise–Mogollon Indians. The most important new element was agriculture. As was suggested in the preceding chapter, corn was probably present as early as 2000 to 4000 B.C., but until adequate storage facilities could be provided so that some corn could be saved for winter consumption and some for planting in the following spring, one could not expect this people to depend completely on an agricultural economy. On the other hand, storage facilities to protect the corn from weather and rodents could not be adequately provided without a sedentary type of life and fixed villages. Therefore, these essentials had to come into being more or less simultaneously. At least that is what we suppose, and present evidence supports our view.

We know next to nothing about the houses or villages (if they existed) in very early times. The earliest type of habitation dates from about 500 B.C. This was a pit-house—a neatly excavated hole, roundish, from ten to sixteen feet in diameter and from two to five feet deep, over which a roof of poles, brush and sod could be constructed. Wind, rain, and snow were excluded by attaching to the main covering of the house a long passage-entrance similar to those of Eskimo igloos. Pit-houses have a long history, with possible connections between the Mogollon area, portions of Siberia, and parts of Europe, where they may have been built 25,000 years ago.

Skeleton found under floor of pit-house. Near the skull lies a small cooking pot; near the ribs are portions of a painted bowl. About A.D. 900.

MORTAR AND PESTLE
About 100 B.C.

Tools of stone: *Left*, maul (about A.D. 200); *right*, three-quarter grooved axe (about A.D. 1000).

Most of the earliest houses (300 B.C. to A.D. 500) were provided with some sort of entryway at the side of the house. The roof was either an umbrella type, the beams of which were supported mainly by a large central upright post, or a flat or domed type, the beams of which were supported by marginal posts. All the roofs were made of thick logs covered by small branches which were coated with heavy layers of mud plaster. Large food-storage pits in the floor were common.

The later pit-houses (A.D. 500 to 1000) tended to be basically rectangular and more carefully excavated and finished on the inside. Most of them were equipped with a side-entryway. Some of these entryways were ramps that sloped upward to the outside ground level. The roofs were generally held up by four or more sturdy upright posts, but the framework and construction were the same as in the earlier houses. The fire hearth—usually a depression in or near the center of the floor —became more frequently a part of the household "equipment." And there were other house furnishings: beds of grass, blankets made of rabbit fur or bird feathers, scouring pads made of plant fibers for cleaning pots and metates, torches of fibers, tongs, fire drills for making fire, and flexible cradles. Food-storage pits became less common in the later pit-houses, perhaps because pottery jars were more abundant and may have been used for food containers.

VILLAGE PATTERNS

In the earliest villages these houses were grouped in a haphazard way, without any particular plan. Usually, such villages were placed in isolated spots and often high up on a ridge or mesa that could be defended. Forested, mountainous areas well removed from streams were preferred spots. Some of the early communities were sizable. One such excavated by us, the SU site, contained at least 26 pit-houses. Nearness to land suitable for farming may have been one factor in selecting a site for the village. In almost every village containing more than 3 or 4 pit-houses there is a larger pit-house that was probably used for ceremonies and religious rituals.

It is barely possible that the earliest towns were abandoned seasonally, perhaps in the winter, although we do not know where the inhabitants went. Certainly many of the early houses lack hearths or evidence of any fire-area within the house, although many houses have been found with hearths outside. One would think that a pit-house without some fire for warmth would be gloomy and cold in the winter, especially in the mountains at an altitude of 6,500 feet.

If the Mogollon Indians were wont to disperse seasonally— and this is only a guess—is it not possible that this habit may have been conserved for a long time and may account for the ease with which towns dated after A.D. 1000 were changed, modified, broken up into new and separate units and moved a short distance away?

Villages assigned to the later part of this emergent period were built without any observable plan. Houses were placed near one another wherever it was convenient to dig them.

FLEXIBLE CRADLE WITH GRASS BEDDING
About 300 B.C.

91

RECONSTRUCTION OF TOWN SHOWN
ON OPPOSITE PAGE
About A.D. 1000

AN EARLY TOWN OR PUEBLO

Showing remains of lowest courses of masonry and cellular arrangement
of rooms that were probably one story in height (about A.D. 1000).

The preferred location for the village was on a ridge or mesa, although some communities have been found on lower terraces or near small streams.

No village or community as large as the SU site of 26 pit-houses was observed for the later part of this epoch. Usually, one finds that a village contained from 5 to 15 houses.

Pit structures (kivas) set aside for ritualistic purposes and ceremonies are ordinarily found associated with each of the larger villages. These special houses are larger and more carefully finished on the interior, and they usually have some other features, such as foot drums, floor grooves, or large fire-pits, that distinguish them from the secular houses.

Although each village was independent, the one possessing a kiva was probably a "ceremonial center." It seems probable that several villages united for special rituals and important feast days. If their social and religious organization resembled that of contemporary pueblos, it is likely that a small village was not necessarily blessed with a full consistory of priests; therefore, for special religious events, the services of priests of several villages would have been required to perform a complete service.

FAMILY LIFE

In the previous chapter, I explained briefly that the Mogollon habit of food-collecting in a limited area probably made permanent habitations and food-storage reservoirs more or less impossible. Furthermore, the practice of food-collecting would have effectively prevented the establishment of large family groups and the formation of villages and of large communal gatherings other than occasional ones.

Hence, it seemed to follow that the earlier Mogollones (pre-500 B.C.) would have fallen into small simple bands, the mother, father and children constituting a nuclear family. I guess, on the basis of contemporary peoples in a similar situation, that descent was reckoned through both sides of the family, but that the women collected all the food and owned the food patches and the houses. It is also probable that the

Early type of footgear: a four warp wickerwork sandal (about 300 B.C. or earlier). The toe goes through the loop, and the string ties around the ankle.

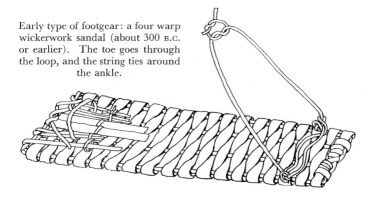

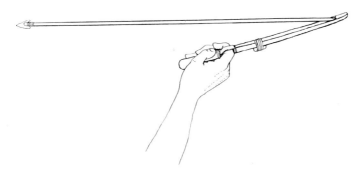

Spear thrower (atlatl) and spear, showing method of casting. This type of weapon was used in hunting small and large game and was the principal weapon known to the Mogollon Indians from early times to about A.D. 500. The bow and arrow were introduced at this time and the spear thrower went completely out of style (about A.D. 900).

daughters of the household brought their husbands to live in the mother's house. This is called "matrilocal residence."

But in this emergent period, during which houses had been introduced and small towns or communities had sprung into being, the composition of the family and of society would have been somewhat more involved and complex. In this situation, where person-to-person relations are prevalent, family relationships and kinship are a dominant factor. The people of the community would have desired close and constant association with their kin, and a person who left his home folk and drifted away would have been virtually unknown. Therefore, we would expect a strengthening and intensifying of the social factors that existed in the previous era and we assume that the patterns of family organization would have tended to follow the same general path of development with some elaboration.

With the increase in importance of agriculture in this period, matrilocal residence would have been intensified, giving rise to what is called matrilocal extended families: the mother, the father, the unmarried daughters, the married daughters and their husbands and children, and the brothers of the mother. This group, the household, normally occupied a large pit-house or a set of adjacent pit-houses or adjoining rooms which it used in common. The father of the family and the husbands of the married daughters would probably have spent some time in their natal households. In matters regarding rituals, they would have had little to say.

Further, reasoning partly by analogy and partly by knowledge of contemporary families, we would expect that as a result of a matrilocal household, definite descent and inheritance through the mother-line only, would probably have developed by this time. Inheritance of corn plots and of areas yielding wild edible plants (both of these a major form of wealth) would have strengthened the economic position of women and would have favored matrilineal descent. The clans, a group of people united through the female line, probably owned the ceremonies or rituals, and the objects and apparatus used in rituals. These were stored (when not used) in the home of the head woman of the clan.

After A.D. 500, we find villages built in any choice spot and usually not on high, isolated, defendable ridges or mesas. We assume that an era of good will, security, and peace had set in, for the villages were situated in the open, near streams but without an eye to defense. Presumably, lack of enemies permitted the population to spread and perhaps a more stable food supply allowed it to multiply. At any rate, we find an increase in the number of villages in the period from A.D. 600 to 1000.

The change in milling stones (from a basin type to a troughed type) implies that agriculture had largely supplanted the gathering of wild food plants. Hunting may have become more important—a conjecture based on an increase in the ratio of projectile points to milling stones.

I guess that the continuity of the family organization would have flowed on and in more or less the same channels as before; that is, extended families, perhaps several to a village; a requirement that married daughters bring their husbands to live in the mother's house (matrilocal residence); descent reckoned through the mother-line as well as mother-line inheritance; one or more clans (people united through the female line) to a village; each village politically independent; no slavery; no social classes, with the possible exception of an elected head man; and monogamy. A weak inter-village confederation may have existed, on a consulting level only.

CEREMONIALISM; GODS AND SPIRITS

Earlier in this chapter, I mentioned that at the time when houses and villages developed there were also special houses (kivas) that may have been set aside for religious functions. ("Kiva" is a Hopi Indian word that means "old house." The term, in modern usage, means a separate and distinct chamber set aside primarily for ceremonial purposes and secondarily as a clubhouse and lounging place for males.)

The earliest kivas are merely large pit-houses. The features which distinguish what we call kivas from the secular houses are: greater size (they are several times larger than a dwelling); greater depth; floor grooves shaped like half logs, the purpose of which is unknown; and a lack of domestic tools. The floor grooves may have held hollow logs that served as foot drums.

I must admit that these features may not convince one that these large pit-houses were used for ceremonial purposes. I can only say that it is my impression that they *were* kivas. Most archaeologists agree on this tenuous point. I might add that one can see an architectural connection between these early kivas and later buildings that are certainly kivas.

MATERIALS USED IN CEREMONIES

From the early levels of Tularosa Cave we excavated flutes, dice, body paint, paint-grinding stones, crystals, odd-shaped stones, animal claws, juniper-berry skewers, animal and human effigies, reed cigarettes, prayer-sticks, toy bows and arrows, and stone tobacco pipes, all of which were probably used in ceremonies of various kinds. And if ceremonies were in existence—even simple ones—they must have been performed somewhere and probably in a special chamber set aside for communal activities, family prayers, and varied religious services. Hence, we can imagine large pit-houses serving as kivas, especially when we find them lacking in everyday household utensils, and in the burials which are often found under the floors of ordinary houses.

CEREMONIES

If it be granted that the assumptions set forth in the previous paragraphs are reasonable and are based on some tangible evidence, then we may properly make a few guesses concerning the nature of these ceremonies. The guesses will be supported by the nature of the excavated ceremonial paraphernalia and their similarity to contemporary ritualistic objects, and by comparison with contemporary ceremonial systems in the Southwest. I might add here also a parenthetical word about the materials that we label "ceremonial." Most of the things that I listed in the preceding paragraph have no practical value or use, as far as we determine; for example, crystals, odd-shaped stones, animal claws, phallic representations, skewers of wood on which juniper berries had been impaled, zoomorphic effigies—none of these appears to be important or necessary for actual existence and none would have been useful in creating a house, planting a field, harvesting a crop, or hunting. All activities of life could have been successfully pursued without any of these articles.

Corrugated pottery jar used for storage of food or for cooking (about A.D. 1000).

It is possible that a few objects that I call "ceremonial" might have been used purely for amusement or in games: flutes, dice, and toy bows and arrows. The chances are, however, that these, too, had religious uses.

Smoking tobacco, whether in a pipe or a cigarette, was a sacred and solemn rite well-nigh throughout North America. To have used tobacco, then, in any other context appears most unlikely and unacceptable to me. Tobacco pipes were more popular early, but after A.D. 700, reed cigarettes became more fashionable.

To paint parts of the human body, masks, tablitas (head ornaments of wood) and other paraphernalia is routine practice today among many Southwestern Pueblo Indians (the Hopi, especially). It does not seem amiss to me, therefore, to conjecture that these practices have a long history and were part of the cultural heritage handed down to modern Indians by their ancestors, both near and remote. Therefore actual raw pigments and small slabs on which the pigments were reduced to powder would also be classed as ceremonial.

After this digression, I should now like to hazard a few hints as to the ceremonialism of this period. I assume that the religious and sacred rites would be reflected in a general manner in the objects discussed above.

In the earlier part of this period, one would expect the emphasis to be on ceremonies for curing the sick. As agriculture grew in importance, rituals for bringing rain may have been developed. The presence of miniature bows and arrows suggests puberty rites to emphasize a boy's transition from childhood to the adult group and perhaps to initiate the boy into one or more religious societies. Group ceremonies and dances may have been held in kivas featuring masked dancers wearing tablitas and body paint. Such ritualistic dances may have been a re-enactment of the myths of the Mogollones.

Such dramatic performances eventually may have involved the marking of the summer and winter solstices (about June 21 and December 21); and they may have developed into ceremonials for the promotion of precipitation, tribal fecundity, planting and harvesting, and good crops. Emphasis was probably placed on curing and rain-making. Music produced by means of flutes, singing, and drumming was perhaps important.

Psychosomatic medicine is suggested by the finding of a "doctor's" bag containing obsidian flakes, crystals, curiously shaped concretions, toes of a great horned owl, a horn of a rhinoceros beetle, and herbs, including one known today as "cough root." All of these objects—some fifty in all—were tied up in a muskrat skin. This may have been the property of a priest of the curing society.

100

MEDICINE MAN'S POUCH

Pouch made of skin of muskrat (right); contents (left) includes flakes of
obsidian and quartz, concretions, toes of an owl, and vegetable matter.
About A.D. 1100.

METHODS OF BURIAL

The dead were ordinarily buried in pits under the house floors. After interment, the pits were floored over and the family continued to occupy its home. The dead were probably wrapped in skins and mats, and with them were placed mortuary offerings: pottery bowls and jars, jewelry, tools of stone and bone, and perhaps food. From this evidence I surmise that these people believed in the hereafter and in life after death.

Thus, although we have no direct records of ceremonialism, we have abundant, though indirect testimony that a rich and devout religious life had been developed. These people were close to nature—closer than we ever are or can be—and it is probable that they were well versed in the movements of many of the heavenly bodies; that from them they had worked out a crude, seasonal calendar; and that they were well acquainted with terrifying storms, floods, droughts, and other awesome natural manifestations. The very lives they led and their manner of living must have generated fear of nature as well as respect for it, and a certain, indefinable purity and pragmatic, contemplative philosophy.

The BEGINNINGS

of TOWN LIFE

ABOUT A.D. 1000 TO A.D. 1350

The archaeological periods covered in this chapter are known as the Reserve and Tularosa periods. As the reader will have noted, the span of time is astonishingly brief—a mere 300 to 400 years—as compared with a span of 1500 years for the previous stage. One may wonder why there is such a contrast in time; why one period is long and the next, short.

This arrangement is partly an arbitrary and partly a natural one. This grouping seemed to "fit" the facts, because the Reserve and Tularosa periods are essentially similar in many characteristics. Furthermore, as a civilization becomes more mature its "metabolic processes" appear to speed up. All developments are faster; the old conservative ways are swept away by the onrushing stream of events. Culture changes are swifter, because there are more frequent and significant alterations in life conditions.

CEREMONIAL ROOM (GREAT KIVA)
In Reserve–Pine Lawn area (about A.D. 775). Fire hearth and storage
pits in center. Purpose of grooves in floor is not known.

In the previous chapter, I noted certain changes such as the introduction of architecture and pottery-making and the greater dependence on planted crops; but I am sure the reader will sense that alterations and innovations were few and that the way of life jogged along at a comfortable but slow pace.

METHODS OF CULTURAL CHANGE

It might be well to digress briefly to discuss some of the methods by which cultures or civilizations change.

Innovations are frequently brought about when habitual ways of doing things are discouraged and when a significant event occurs that changes the situation to which a people have become accustomed. Some such significant alterations of life conditions may be: (1) an increase in population; (2) a change in climate; (3) a migration into a new environment; (4) contacts (by trade or war) with other people; (5) catastrophes,

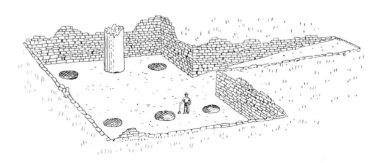

GREAT KIVA IN PROCESS OF EXCAVATION

Area about 1,300 square feet, not including 30-foot ramp. Holes in floor formerly held gigantic upright posts (as suggested in drawing) that supported the massive timber-and-sod roof.

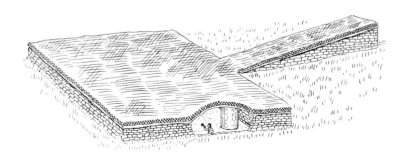

RESTORATION OF GREAT KIVA SHOWN ABOVE

The feature that particularly distinguishes this type of Great Kiva is the roofed, wide ramp entrance at right, through which six ceremonially dressed dancers could have marched abreast in processions. About A.D. 1175. Drawing based on photographs and data obtained by Museum Expeditions.

such as floods or droughts, crop failure, epidemics, or wars; (6) discoveries of new techniques; and (7) the rise of a powerful leader.

But no matter how much or how little previous habitual behavior may be modified, the cultural change will probably not be socially acceptable and will not be taken over by an impressive percentage of the population. Conditions must be just right or an innovation will not "take." In our own society, for example, we find resistance in this country and in England to the adoption of the metric system of linear measurement to replace inches, feet, yards, and the like. Most of the world has adopted this system, which is superior to our irregular Anglo-Saxon one. If we took over metrics, we would then be in step with the international system of measurement and this would make for greater convenience in the future, although there might be confusion for perhaps a generation. I could also cite the attempts to reform our spelling and our calendar, but these, too, have no appeal to our culture.

But cultural change is inevitable. If a culture becomes stagnant and fossilized, it will probably die. In the case of the Mogollon culture, we are aware that innovations were constantly seeping into the framework and that a goodly number appeared between A.D. 500 and 1000; but some were not totally accepted or integrated until about A.D. 1000, when new habits and ways of life were formed and became habitual patterns of behavior. Naturally, this did not happen overnight or precisely at the year 1000, but at about this time we can detect significant differences and changes in the archaeological picture and thus the eleventh century appears to be an important milepost.

The previous span of 1500 years, treated in the preceding chapter, seemed a reasonable one, for the innovations mentioned therein appeared to have been more slowly accepted and the integrated society less disturbed. In other words the situation was relatively more static and the elements that made up that span of 1500 years, during which small sedentary communities evolved, seemed to have disturbed less the pre-existing patterns of behavior. I can think of the span 500 B.C. to A.D. 1000 as a unit and one that is more or less justifiable

View of pueblo after several rooms had been excavated. About A.D. 1175.

for classification purposes of this sort, wherein one has to sort the small grains from the larger masses lest the reader become bogged down in a morass of details.

In general, then, this span of three or four centuries (A.D. 1000 to 1350) is to be regarded as a climax in the his-

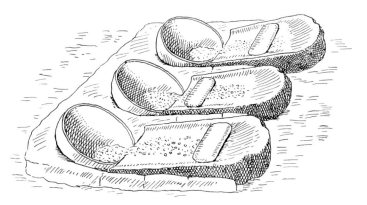

Mealing bins or built-in corn mills consisting of milling stones (coarse, medium and fine), handstones, and pottery bowls placed so as to catch the flour (about A.D. 1200). To obtain powdered flour, the corn was ground successively on the three milling stones. Such mealing bins are found in some Pueblo Indian rooms today.

tory of the Mogollon Indians in the Reserve–Pine Lawn area. Several permanent towns were founded, each as an independent and self-sufficient community, and the population became somewhat greater. If circumstances had not eventually forced the inhabitants to abandon the area and to migrate north and westward, we might have witnessed the growth of large towns and the development of a more advanced civilization.

MAKING A LIVING

In this period, from the eleventh to the fourteenth century, the means for making a living did not differ greatly from those of the preceding centuries, but one would guess that agricultural techniques had been well adapted to the environment so as to make the most of the land. Favorable farm sites that were well watered or adaptable to flood irrigation were probably selected. We also assume that cultivated plants became the primary food source, thus reducing the area needed per person for subsistence and mere maintenance. Cultivated plants also would have provided a dependable surplus, sufficient to release time and energy that could have been expended on leisure, meditation, ceremonies, and specialization in arts and crafts and technological developments. As a result, an incipient guild of artisans may have been evolving.

From an examination of the plant remains, we have discovered that the last inhabitants of the Reserve–Pine Lawn area *were* skillful farmers and must have depended primarily on agriculture for subsistence. The corn they grew was good, and the individual grains were plump and large. Several different kinds of corn were cultivated and they resemble the corn grown until recently by the Pima and Mohave Indians. These types were probably introduced into the Mogollon area some time during the preceding centuries and gradually replaced the earlier, more primitive, and therefore less desirable types. The ears of this late Reserve–Tularosa corn displayed relatively fewer numbers of rows of grain (a sign of more "efficient" types)—perhaps 8 to 10 rows as compared with 12, 14, and 16 rows in earlier times (about the time of Christ). In addition to corn that produced a rich harvest, these people grew kidney and tepary beans, two kinds of squashes, and the bottle gourd.

This evidence warrants the guess that the Mogollon Indians of the eleventh to the fourteenth centuries were successful farmers. There is no indication that the people were undergoing a difficult, food-scarce time. The economy seems healthy as we appraise it with the meager evidence at our command.

Just as we supplement our diet with herbs and special foods, so did the Mogollon Indians add to theirs by gathering and eating wild seeds and greens: walnuts, pigweed, salt brush seeds, wild gourds, pinyon nuts, mutton grass, grapes, tansy mustard, prickly pear, and sunflower seeds.

Corn was undoubtedly planted by means of a digging stick, baskets were utilized for gathering and storing foods, and tumplines were used for transporting burdens of cornstalks and other loads. Deer, wild pigs, antelopes, rabbits, turkeys, and mountain sheep were the more common game foods and were hunted entirely with bows and arrows (the atlatl had gone out of fashion by this time), snares, rabbit nets, and perhaps spears.

PREPARATION OF FOODS

The preparation of foods probably differed little from that of the previous stage. We conjecture that much, if not all, of the cooking was done indoors, as we find hearths and firepits in almost every room. Methods of cooking foods, wild or domesticated, were probably similar to those of earlier periods and to those used today by contemporary Hopi and Zuñi Indians: broiling, boiling, roasting, baking in ashes, and parching corn and other seeds.

Boiled foods were prepared in pottery jars manufactured especially for this purpose. These cooking pots are called "corrugated" pots because the original coils of manufacture were not obliterated. Food was also stored in corrugated pottery and perhaps in painted bowls and pitchers. Food may have been served in painted or "smudged" bowls, one bowl to a family. Each person probably dipped a finger or a piece of corn bread into the pot and abstracted a mouthful. Knives, forks and spoons and other such refinements were unknown to these people as they were to our ancestors of only a few centuries back. Salt may have been extracted from salty soil deposits or secured by means of trade from the salt lakes in the vicinity of Zuñi.

UTILIZATION AND PROCESSING OF RAW MATERIALS

The remarks in the previous chapter concerning the utilization and processing of raw materials would certainly hold for this period. Many of the natural available resources were seized upon for man's use.

TYPES OF TOOLS

All tools were better made and were sometimes reduced in size. The workmanship was, on the whole, improved. Pro-

Pottery bowl with smudged interior and fillet rim exterior and white-line decoration (about A.D. 1250).

Red, black and white (polychrome) glaze bowl from late "town" (about A.D. 1300).

Polychrome pottery bowl (about A.D. 1200); colors, black and white on red background. Bear paws on outside.

jectile points were smaller and there were two principal types: one had notches on the sides, ear-like barbs, and a concave base; the other was a small triangular point with side notches and saw-tooth edge. Large spear points were also made. Metates were more precisely made and were open at both

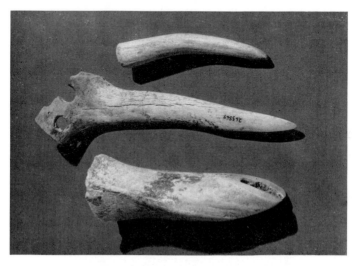

HANDYMAN'S KIT

Top, a flaker of antler for chipping stone tools (about A.D. 1300). *Middle*, a combination awl and wrench for straightening shafts of spindle whorls (about A.D. 1200). *Bottom*, a bone chisel (about A.D. 1200).

ends. Scrapers, choppers and flake knives that occurred in this era are practically indistinguishable from those found at much earlier sites. A few new tool-types were made: beveled manos, small triangular, side-notched arrow points, rectangular arrow-shaft tools and rectangular stone bowls.

Full-grooved and three-quarters grooved axes both occurred in this period for the first time. It is believed at present that the full-grooved type came from the north (the Anasazi country) and that the three-quarters grooved type came from the south, possibly from Hohokam territory.

Drills, saws, abrading stones, paint palettes, worked slabs, hammerstones, and grooved mauls—all of stone—comprised a

112

partial inventory of the tool cabinet of the town dweller of the day.

About twenty different types of stone tools have been tabulated, including, of course, milling stones of several types, pestles, mortars, polishing stones and stone hoes. Some of the

Milling stone used for grinding corn to flour.
About A.D. 1200.

most extraordinary items made of stone include a circular slab bearing a "sun symbol" design in black, red, green, and yellow; a tubular pipe painted in stripes of the same colors; and two animal effigies (possibly a bear and a mountain lion) painted in rainbow arcs of the same colors. These important and perhaps indescribably sacred objects were without any doubt paraphernalia used in rituals.

Tough, resistant volcanic rock, such as basalt or rhyolite, was used for making manos, pestles, metates, slabs, hammerstones and mauls. Chalcedony, flint, jasper and obsidian were the rocks most commonly used in manufacturing projectile and spear points, saws, gravers, knives and other tools that were produced and edged by means of chipping. The circular slab painted to represent the sun was made from sandstone; the pipe and the two stone bowls, from tuff.

CARPENTER'S TOOLS OF STONE

Upper, smooth saw (about A.D. 1100); *lower left,* knife (about A.D. 1000); *center,* toothed saw (about A.D. 1000); *lower right,* drill (about 300 B.C.).

CORDAGE, TEXTILES, BASKETS

While little in the way of cordage, textiles, knots, or clothing has been recovered from late sites (unless charred, these objects decay without trace), we assume that the same classes or kinds of materials were being made and used. Actually, a few charred remains have been recovered and these yield a few clues.

Four charred pieces of fiber cordage were found on the floors of burned rooms. Two of these were made of hair fiber and two of material too fragile to identify. These may have been skeins of string, or they may have been parts of netting, string aprons, or sashes. There were also fragments of cloth

114

of plain weave, probably of cotton; of blankets of fur or feather cloth; of several kinds of basketry; and of matting.

These fragile remains, together with the fragments that we discovered in dry caves, lead me to believe that the inventory of items manufactured from plants was as large as in the preceding period, if not larger. And I also assume that the same materials were used, namely, cotton, bast fibers, hair fibers, yucca, and rushes.

WOODEN TOOLS

We have no wooden artifacts from open sites, because such tools would perish from dampness, but from caves we have recovered enough to warrant the guess that wooden tools did exist in towns out in the open and that they were well made and abundant.

Probably most of the native woods were used—oak, pine, willow, mountain mahogany, and juniper.

A glance around the rooms of a Mogollon village of about A.D. 1300 would have revealed such tools as bows and arrows, digging sticks, trowels, scoops, spoons, stone knives hafted with wooden handles, wooden awls, lapboards, weaving tools and perhaps wooden dice.

BONE TOOLS

Time is kinder to bone tools than to wooden or woven things and thus we have a fair assemblage of bone tools to study. Punches, arrowhead flakes, fleshers, weaving tools, beads, pendants, gaming pieces and bone tubes were the commonest items. Deer bones were mostly used, although occasionally one notes bird, mountain sheep, antelope, and bison bones.

JEWELRY

Bracelets were the favorite jewelry. These were cut and carved from bivalve shells collected in the Gulf of California. Some beads and pendants were also carved from these shells.

Turquoise and lignite were brought into the area by trade for use in ceremonies and in ornaments.

POTTERY TYPES AND MATERIALS

From the native clays a great variety of pottery was made. Some new types came into existence and a few of the older ones began to decline in fashionable usage. The plain brown and plain red wares (Alma Plain and San Francisco Red) occurred, but they were fading in popularity as were the neck corrugated and the incised corrugated types. The indented corrugated pottery was fast replacing some of the earlier textured wares. Another type that was becoming fashionable was a pottery type consisting entirely of bowl forms with a shiny black interior and a brown-black exterior, and embellished with a few coils or fillets on the exterior of the rim (Tularosa fillet rim).

The greatest change took place in the painted decorated types. The red on white ware completely disappeared and in its place we find a black on white pottery that was probably locally made but inspired by Anasazi (or Pueblo Indian) art styles. The paste or clay of the pots was white or gray instead of brown or pink; the pots were covered by a wash of white or gray clay; and the paint used for composing the designs was made from iron-oxide mineral.

There was also a greater variety in shapes in the painted ware. In addition to bowls, one finds pitchers, jars, and ladles, and, in the latter part of this period, canteen-shaped jars, effigy-vessels made to represent ducks and mountain sheep, and a few so-called eccentric forms. The painted types are called Reserve black on white and Tularosa black on white.

Traces of an extraordinarily beautiful pottery type known as Mimbres black on white turned up in many of the sites of this period. The great bulk of Mimbres black on white pottery occurs in the Mimbres Valley in southern New Mexico. The designs on this ware were derived from earlier Mogollon pottery designs, but at and after A.D. 1000 the designs on the Mimbres pottery became increasingly complex, better and more delicately executed, and astonishingly handsome. Many of the designs depict animals, people, and realistic scenes. It may safely be said that Mimbres pottery is among the finest ever created by American Indians.

On the basis of present evidence we guess that the few Mimbres pots that we found in the Pine Lawn–Reserve area

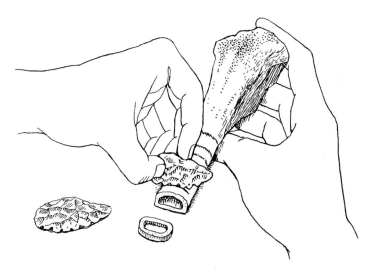

Stone saw being used to produce bone rings (about A.D. 1300).

were brought in by trade, although they may have been locally made.

When the Anasazi-inspired black on white pottery seized the fancy of the Mogollon Indians they almost ceased importing the fine Mimbres pots and went all out for the new craze—Reserve black on white and Tularosa black on white. We are not surprised then to find little if any Mimbres influence on the later, Anasazi-style pots.

In villages that spanned the later part of the period under discussion, we found a red ware decorated with black paint (black on red ware). This is a pleasing type. After a time, another color, white, was added to the designs on this black on red ware. This type has been dubbed St. Johns polychrome. This type became very popular and spread over

117

many parts of the southwest during its life span of some 200 to 300 years. Whether this black on red ware was made locally is not known, but certainly many of the designs are the same as those on the contemporary, sister ware, Tularosa black on white.

Just before the area was abandoned, glaze-paint polychrome ware, derived directly from St. Johns polychrome, was imported.

Instead of trying to describe the details of any of these pots I shall rely on illustrations to make clear what I am talking about. I think it is evident that the Mogollon peoples of the thirteenth century possessed great dexterity in the manipulation of clays and in the texturing, painting and firing of pottery. These skills are partially reflected in the fact that approximately twelve pottery types were made in the thirteenth century, about seven of which were utility or cooking-pot types.

Judging by the soot on the pottery found, we think that the favorite types used in cooking were the corrugated or textured jars and the smudged bowls. The favorite types used mostly for storage and serving of food were the fillet-rim and the textured or corrugated bowls. The eccentric and effigy vessels may have been used primarily for ritualistic purposes and they appear to have been the property of the female line, as they are associated with female skeletons.

It should be noted that ladles were rare; mugs were wholly absent; and jars were the commonest type.

HOUSES AND SETTLEMENT PATTERNS

The title of this chapter is *The Beginnings of Town Life*. This seemed to be a likely name for this stage of Mogollon development, because fairly large towns or centers of population came into existence. These were self-supporting units and may have encouraged the growth of smaller, satellite hamlets. The larger towns usually included a Great Kiva or ceremonial center that may have served nearby smaller towns which could not or did not support such a center.

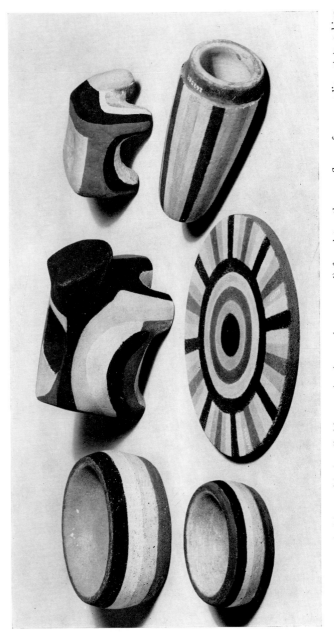

Painted ceremonial objects of indescribable sanctity (somewhat restored) found together on floor of room adjacent to a kiva. Mortars, animal effigies, tubular tobacco pipe and a "sun disc." Colors are black, red, green and yellow. These objects resemble ritualistic objects found in modern Indian pueblos. About A.D. 1200.

119

A Mogollon "town" was almost always erected near a stream or a good spring; usually it was built on a flat plain near a stream or on a terrace just above the flood plain or on a knoll near the river or spring. Defense of these towns was probably not necessary, as most of them lack walls, moats, or steep approaches. There they were, out on a plain or a gentle rise—and a sitting duck for an enemy host had there been one.

The town itself was a kind of cellular structure, composed of a number of contiguous rooms, built on the surface of the ground (as opposed to pit-houses); each apartment or set of family rooms was furnished with a private entrance, as they are in our apartment buildings. The whole mass of rooms, varying in number from 30 to 50, was fairly well planned before construction, although additions and alterations were frequently made. We guess that parts of the town were two stories high, perhaps even three, and that the population was perhaps from 100 to 500 people. The rooms ranged in size from 6 by 6 feet to 15 by 16 feet. Some were nearly square, while others were rectangular. Many of the larger towns were built around a court or plaza that was roofed; sometimes a low retaining wall on one side enclosed a good-sized area that formed a patio or plaza.

Situated close to the town was the Great Kiva, the center of community worship and the scene of important festivals and ceremonies. Entrance to the Kiva chamber was by means of a ramp, 10 feet wide and 33 feet long.

CONSTRUCTION OF HOUSES

Earlier, I stated that rooms were built on top of the ground. Surface construction implies the use of walls built up to the desired height and composed of adobe, stone, brick, or logs. The towns of this stage of Mogollon development were different from the clusters of pit-houses mentioned in an earlier chapter. At first the walls of the buildings consisted of masonry made up of unshaped river cobbles; later they were improved by including laminated slabs or rough, shaped blocks of stone. Mud served as mortar. Such walls were erected on the surface of the ground, sometimes on a special

BLACK-ON-WHITE POTTERY JAR AND STONE BOWLS
FROM A PUEBLO, AND SACRED, PAINTED STONES FROM A
GREAT KIVA. ABOUT A.D. 1175–1200

footing or foundation, and were built or abutted one against another or bonded one to another in such a way as to form a series of outer walls and partition walls, thus creating a "town" (a series of contiguous surface rooms).

MASONRY

It is probable that the Mogollon Indians did not devise stone masonry. It seems likely that the notion of building stone walls was borrowed from the Anasazi Indians to the north. Hence, it is assumed that the idea of a cellular structure—a pueblo or town of contiguous rooms—was also borrowed from Pueblo Indians. I should add that at the time that these ideas concerning architecture were gaining vogue the ideas of making black on white painted pottery and other traits to be mentioned later were also adopted from the Anasazi.

GREAT KIVA AND THE PLAZA

Although we have noted the influx of new traits from the north, it should be added that building around a court or a plaza may have been a Mogollon contribution; certainly the Great Kiva with ramp entrance was the result of Mogollon inspiration.

PIT STRUCTURES

Curiously enough, in these large towns with contiguous surface rooms of masonry, we find that pit structures were also being contemporaneously built and used. These pits were rectangular (about 10 by 12 feet, with the floor about 5 feet below the surface), were roofed over, and were lined with masonry walls. Floors were of adobe plaster and let into them were stone-lined firepits. Ventilation was provided by fresh-air ducts, the shafts of which ran up to the surface. When a fire was lighted the smoke and warm air drifted up and out through the hatchway in the roof. This upward motion drew cool fresh air down the ventilator shaft and into the pit room. Such ventilating devices were common in all Anasazi kivas and earlier Anasazi pit-houses. Similar but less well-devel-

Effigy of mountain sheep (?) made of black-on-white pottery. About A.D. 1200.

Black-on-white pottery pitcher. About A.D. 1200.

Black-on-white pottery ladle. About A.D. 1200.

123

oped devices probably obtained in Mogollon pit-houses, in which the lateral entryway served as a ventilator shaft. The Anasazi probably deserve credit for perfecting this device and making it neat and shipshape and finished in appearance.

On the floors of many of these pit structures one finds corn-grinding mills or metate bins permanently affixed to the floor, usually three in a set, separated from one another by means of a thin stone partition. A very rough metate was placed at one end to produce a coarse grind; a less rough one in the middle for a medium-coarse grind; and a smoothly textured one at the opposite end for a very fine grind or a powdered flour. Each metate was tilted the long way, and at the lower end of each one and depressed slightly into the floor was a pottery bowl, usually smudged ware, to catch the flour as it was ground up by the mano or handstone that was vigorously rubbed up and down on the metate (see figure, p. 108).

These built-in corn mills and flour-catching receptacles are referred to in the archaeological "trade jargon" as mealing bins.

Thus, most of these late pit structures were provided with firepits, ventilators, mealing bins, manos, and flour receptacles. The function of these subterranean structures is not certainly known. In form, they resemble the pit-houses of the previous centuries (rectangular shape). The ventilator apparatus and the mealing bins may have been features introduced from the Anasazi tribes to the north, although these points are moot. At the present time it is assumed that the pit structures were domiciles that served also as places for family worship or lesser ceremonies.

It is not surprising to find that pit structures survived up to the fourteenth century, for they have been found in the later Anasazi villages also. Just what kind of social organization the presence of surface as well as subterranean structures implies I don't know. We have no contemporary examples to draw on for explanation. Perhaps the conservatives lived in the pit dwellings and the progressives in the surface pueblos; perhaps the pit-houses served as winter dwellings; perhaps the presence of pit-houses was an expression of a guild or priestly division, with the general population living in the surface rooms and members of a guild or the priesthood living in the pit-houses; perhaps the families that guarded the sacred ceremonial objects felt obliged to live in an "old-time" type of house and thus inhabited the pit structures; perhaps the difference in house types was due merely to individual preference —with some people feeling warmer and snugger and less subject to attacks of rheumatism(!) in pit-houses. We really do not know the answers at present.

HOUSE INTERIORS

Although the houses of this phase are "better" if judged by our standards, it must be remembered that the interiors probably represented the utmost in Spartan simplicity. The interior and exterior walls were plastered with adobe. The walls of some rooms may have been embellished with simple painted decorations, similar to those found on pottery. The household furnishings were of the simplest order: beds of grass covered with skins or blankets of rabbit fur or feathers, pots, scouring pads made of plant fibers, metates and manos or mealing bins, torches of cedar bark, fire drills for making fire, fire tongs, flexible cradles, baskets, perhaps a loom and perhaps some ears of corn. Netted carrying bags, burden straps, and flexible carrying baskets may have hung on wall pegs. There was no furniture in our sense of the word. Certainly there were no chairs of any kind. One squatted on one's heels or sat cross-legged on a mat or skin on the floor. Even today, the houses of Hopi and Zuñi Indians are sparsely furnished, although the more acculturated Indians own chairs, beds, tables, and sewing machines.

PLAZAS OR COURTS

The larger and later towns, as mentioned above, looked inward. The rooms faced a plaza or plazas. There were no rows of houses, no streets. Each pueblo was a large block of rooms. The Anasazi towns of this period tended to look outward or have an outward-facing appearance. Their blocks of rooms were often built in a semi-circle or in straight rows of rooms with "streets" between the rows.

125

The Mogollon type of village plan undoubtedly reflects the mental attitudes of the people. Perhaps their mode of existence and their ancient isolation in mountain valleys tended to make them introspective and to shape their world outlook.

THE FAMILY

The organization of the family and society was probably the same as that described in some detail in the preceding chapter. Indeed, we can see no cause for major shifts. I should merely expect intensification of various features of kinship, rules of residence, and clan organization. The emphasis was matrilineal, and matrilocal residence was probably the rule. The matrilineal household consisted of a woman and her husband, her married daughters and their husbands, her unmarried children, and the children of her married daughters. The women comprised the important part of the unit because they owned the house, prepared and disbursed the food, and cared for the religious paraphernalia. This extended household probably occupied a series of adjacent rooms.

The clan—a group of people united or related through the female line—probably grew in importance and may have assumed more important functions. Each clan probably owned certain lands for the use of its members. Control of particular ceremonies was probably in the keeping of a particular clan.

PATTERNS OF COMMUNITY LIFE

I shall summarize here my conjectures concerning the patterning of community life in the Reserve area between A.D. 1000 and 1350.

Each town was economically and politically independent, but in times of danger several villages probably banded together for joint action. Discussion, visits, counseling and inter-marriage between villages was probably common.

Each town was probably divided into a series of matrilineal clans united and sharing a totemic animal. Each clan was composed of one or more mother-lines. Matrilocal residence and extended families living in adjacent rooms were the rule. There was probably some emphasis on village organization along clan lines. In addition, there may have been kiva groups and men's societies concerned with tribal initiation rights, winter and summer solstice ceremonies, rain-making, and ceremonies for war and for curing the sick. All rituals were probably organized in terms of a ceremonial calendar. Political authority was probably in the hands of a council of priests with one man acting as the head of the hierarchy.

The principal matters that came before the council probably related to appointments for secular offices; the choice of impersonators of various deities or gods; the choice of a time for tribal initiations; any proposed changes in the ceremonial calendar; and general questions of tribal policy.

The whole welfare of the town was in the hands of this council, which may or may not have concerned itself with secular quarrels and problems, or with crimes. These latter were probably dealt with directly by the family or families or by a small unit of the clan.

Thus the pattern of family and social organization may have given rise to that which obtains today among the western Pueblo Indians.

CEREMONIALISM; GODS AND SPIRITS

Ceremonialism of a complex sort may be safely inferred for this period because ceremonial objects and ceremonial rooms or kivas have been discovered. Since these objects and buildings bear specific resemblances to those used in the sixteenth century and in contemporary Hopi and Zuñi Indian societies, we are probably not far off in our surmises. In fact, we can speak with a fair amount of accuracy, because the contemporary ceremonies, religious beliefs and practices of the Hopi and Zuñi Indians were not created today or yesterday; they yield certain internal evidences of some antiquity. This being so, it does not require too much imagination to conceptualize these earlier rituals and beliefs. The ceremonialism and the ritualistic organizations of the Mogollon Indians of A.D. 1200, for example, are not far removed in time or space from those

127

witnessed by the Spaniards in 1540 and afterward, and by recent observers. It is probable that the rituals and beliefs of the Roman Catholic religion have undergone few changes in the last 500 years. And so, probably, have the principal religious concepts of the Hopis and Zuñis also remained largely unchanged.

I assume, then, that the ceremonialism of the Mogollones was highly developed and that religion or many aspects of it pervaded all activities. It is also probable that ceremonialism had rich and harmonious forms that were externalized in rituals, prayers, and offerings. Ritual was mainly a device for controlling the supernatural; and there was a strong feeling against despoiling or taking advantage of the forests, streams, fields, and animals—all considered manifestations of the supernatural.

Many of the rituals were supposed to remind the supernatural forces—the Sun, the Moon, the Katchinas (ancestral spirits), the Rain Maker, the Beast Spirits and the War "Gods"—that man is dependent upon their generosity. Offerings such as food, tobacco, prayer meal (a coarsely ground corn meal containing bits of shell and turquoise), prayer-sticks, and sacrifices (animal and possibly human) were all used to help influence the supernatural forces. Other accessories such as fetishes, masks, altars, stone images of the Beast Spirits, amulets, paint, sand paintings, embroidered white cotton kilts, embroidered sashes (depicted on Mimbres and Hopi pottery), fox tails, gourd rattles, copper bells worn as anklets or wristlets, shell and turquoise necklaces, ceremonial bows and arrows, feathered wands and staves, polished stone implements, feather boxes, drums, and flutes, were venerated in ceremonies and were also employed in controlling the supernatural forces.

DEVELOPMENT OF CALENDAR

A ceremonial calendar probably determined the dates for the ceremonies. This calendar was one that had slowly evolved during the previous centuries and had been handed down by oral tradition from generation to generation. Being farmers, the Mogollon Indians must have observed the passing of the seasons, the times of rain and snows, and the apparent movement of the sun from north to south and then back again. Apparently the winter and summer solstices were fairly important to them and from these two fixed dates all other ceremonies were dated. Just how the date of the solstice was calculated by observation is not known. By noting the rising or setting posi-

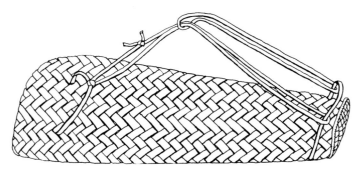

A plaited sandal (about A.D. 1200).

tions of the sun with reference to certain landmarks, they may have been able to determine, for example, whether the sun was still moving southward or whether that journey had been halted and the sun was starting to move northward again. Thus the solstices could have been fixed with relative accuracy.

It is barely possible that the idea of reckoning time and the methods for fixing certain important dates were diffused to the Mogollon Indians from Meso-America, where, as we well know, accurate calendars had been devised, eclipses foretold, and systems of counting the days evolved. And most of these data had been written down!

We do not know, then, whether the Mogollones devised their own calendar independently of their cousins in Meso-America or whether they were helped by their cousins. But an "oral" calendar probably existed. (Today, the position of the sun at sunset time with reference to the San Francisco Peaks, Flagstaff, Arizona, is carefully observed daily by a Hopi priest.) At any rate, the dates for planting, for rain-making ceremonies, for giving thanks to the proper supernatural forces for good crops, and for holding most ritualistic observances were set by the tribal calendar. There could be no deviation.

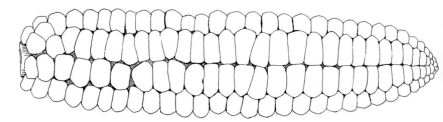

Late ear of corn of the type grown about A.D. 1300–1400.
Length about 5 inches.

PURPOSES OF CEREMONIES

In many of the ceremonies, part of the community may have served as audience. The elaborate public ceremonies, which usually followed the esoteric rituals, were colorful, exciting, dramatic events and were probably looked forward to with boundless enthusiasm, just as today some of us enjoy watching great spectacles: parades, Rose-Bowl games, baseball games, county and state fairs, and super-gigantic movies.

The ceremonies, both the secret and private portions and the public displays and dances, were usually directed toward community goals of recognized and accepted value such as bringing rain or snow, producing abundant harvests, making game and plant life more plentiful, increasing the fertility of the tribe, curing sicknesses, assuring victory over enemies, compelling the sun by magical methods to turn its course northward or southward (the solstice ceremonies), and managing the tribal initiation rites. The *life crises* ceremonies, such as rituals concerned with birth, puberty, marriage and death, tended to become less important.

Predominant in the ceremonial orthodoxy was the belief that all natural objects possessed a soul (animistic doctrine) and the worship of ancestors and individuals or classes of beings who influenced human affairs. These beings probably included Katchinas (the spirits of the ancestors), the Sun, the Earth, Corn, Preying Animals (the Mountain Lion, the Bear, the Badger, the Gopher), and Spirits having to do with war. At the root of the religion was a fervent worship of the spirits of all the ancestors who were believed to visit the towns from time to time and to take an interest in the welfare of their descendants, and, if properly venerated, to help the earth peoples in time of distress.

The religion, then, was not personal, as is ours, but consisted of a series of participations in group rituals. It was a matter for the whole town to be interested in.

Masks were undoubtedly worn (representations of masked dances appear on pottery after A.D. 1100) and are worn today in many Hopi and Zuñi ceremonies. It may have been thought that wearing a mask permitted an ordinary mortal to represent the corporeal substance of an ancestral spirit, and in wearing it, the wearer, through a miracle akin to that of transubstantiation in many religions, became temporarily the ancestral spirit or Katchina.

The elaborate public ceremonies were probably held in the roofed plaza, which was centrally located, or in a suitable place nearby. The secret parts of the rituals, from which most of the public were excluded, were probably held in the kivas.

The term "kiva" is reserved for a place that was set aside for ceremonial use. The kiva was usually semi-subterranean and was equipped with special features. Some of these, in small house-kivas, were described in the last chapter.

STRUCTURE AND USES OF GREAT KIVAS

In this period of A.D. 1000 to 1350 we find not only the smaller, subterranean house-kivas but also the Great Kiva. Great Kivas possessed something rather magnificent in their conception. We know they were large, but we can only guess at the richness of their furnishings and embellishments. Not every village was endowed with such extraordinary structures, but apparently the large and wealthy(?) ones were. Such large buildings indicate a pool of labor that could be drawn on for communal projects and a political organization and central authority that could command these resources. Certainly, planning and bossing a large crew would have been necessary.

Great Kivas of the Mogollon were rectangular and measured approximately 33 by 37 feet or roughly 1,300 square feet. This size creates a room of noble proportions, especially when one remembers that the ceiling, for Indian architecture, was lofty, being from six to eight feet high, and massive.

Perhaps the most interesting feature of the building was the ramp-entryway. As the term implies, this was a sloping floor that led gently downward from the outside ground level to the floor of the ritual chamber. The ramps varied in width and length from village to village, but they averaged about 8 feet wide and from 25 to 30 feet long. They faced eastward. As far as I know, ramp-entryways are confined to Mogollon Great Kivas. The Great Kivas of the Anasazi, borrowed from the Mogollon culture, were circular and were entered by a narrow set of steps.

Now, a ramp entrance of this kind is an interesting architectural feature, but from our point of view it has some disadvantages. One of these is that a considerable volume of water could enter the kiva by this route during a heavy rain storm; and the second is that it would be harder to shut out the drafts of cold air that would blow down such an opening. In other words, putting a door on such an opening would be difficult. Therefore, either the Mogollon Indians used this sacred structure only in warm, dry weather, or they did not give a hoot about cold drafts, or they had devised some suitable means of effectively closing the entrance.

But why construct such a nuisance? The answer, I think, lies in the fact that these long, wide entryways were especially built to accommodate religious processions of priests that marched into or out of these kivas. What a colorful and impressive sight these must have been with priests and participants masked and brightly robed accompanied by musicians playing on flutes, drums, and rattles!

Inside, in the floor, and adjacent to the four gigantic upright posts (from 3 to 4 feet in diameter) that supported the flat timber, brush, and adobe roof, were two grooves or depressions. These, if covered with planks, may have served as foot-drums. In the center, between the grooves, was a large hearth.

The walls may have been plastered and lavishly decorated with paintings of geometrical designs or possibly of mythical beasts in imaginary scenes.

We assume that the nearby satellite villages were served by the Great Kivas and in them were held rituals and possibly sacrifices and feasts of extraordinary sanctity. Such rituals would have required a full consistory of priests, some of whom may have come from adjacent towns. It is barely possible that toward the end of this era, a full consistory of priests might have been lacking, as some of the towns might have been abandoned, thereby creating a situation in which some major ceremonies could not have been performed. This, in turn, may have been another cause that hastened the evacuation of the area, because without the proper ceremonies the people would have felt that life could not be successful.

RITUALS OF BURIAL AND MOURNING

We are uncertain as to the relationship between death, burial, and belief in the supernatural. Among present-day Hopi Indians, the ritual of burial and the mourning for the deceased are restrained and simple in character. Burial takes place as soon as possible. Interred with the body are foods and water for use in the spirit world. It is barely possible that the rituals concerning death and burial were somewhat more involved for the Mogollon Indians of the twelfth and thirteenth centuries. Among contemporary Hopi, the cemetery is at the foot of the hill on which they live. Among the Mogollones, burial took place under the floor of the house (an old Mogollon custom) or in the nearby trash midden. The deceased was wrapped in a deerskin robe, and mortuary offerings such as pottery, jewelry, tools of stone or bone, and food were placed in the grave. Sometimes as many as 22 pots were buried with one individual.

From the fact that the burials were close to or inside of the pueblo, I think that the ritual of burial must have been charged with some emotional elements and that the deceased was longed for rather than put out of mind. Perhaps it was believed that the individual did not really die—that he returned to the underworld whence he came and where he would carry on specialized activities. It is possible that the quantity of mortuary offerings depended on the status of the deceased. In general, the pottery interred with children tended to be of poor quality and was often miniature in size.

We can picture the towns of the thirteenth and fourteenth centuries as forming a peaceful farming society that was somewhat isolated from other Southwestern tribes by geographic features. Perhaps rainfall was never too abundant and agriculture could be successful only by means of great perseverance, collaboration, and teamwork. Abundant rains and a good crop were of inordinate value and were the prime factors in keeping this civilization alive. These two factors—rain and crops—made the people realize how dependent they were on nature and this dependence was probably the cause of the people's religious attitude toward the forces of nature; hence, prayers and ceremonies that concerned themselves primarily with these essentials, and a religion that was directed towards appeasing nature so that the rains would fall!

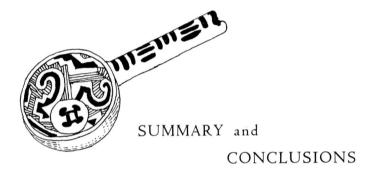

SUMMARY and
CONCLUSIONS

In this book I have presented a brief history of a group of Indians whom we call the Mogollon. I have tried to set forth the major stages of their development as revealed by the excavation and study of material objects and their associations. It is prehistory, because I have given the details of the different cultural traits as they occurred and the approximate dates at which they appeared. In so doing, I was interested in seeking explanations of why and how this particular culture or civilization developed. In this latter aim, I can only suggest a few explanations, as the significant causes still elude me. But before dealing with this subject I should like briefly to review the various levels of development—the evolutionary stages, if you will.

135

THE EARLIEST STAGE

The earliest level or era, some 10,000 years ago, was one in which the ancestors of the Mogollon Indians along with others of the Desert Area were eking out an existence by collecting wild food plants and hunting small game. In a sense these Mogollon ancestors moving about in the valleys and mountains of the Southwest were destined to become farmers because they were experienced in gathering wild foods and in observing the ways of plant life, and because they depended on a crop of wild foods—seeds, nuts, berries, and bulbs—for subsistence. When they obtained, probably by contact, the knowledge of planting maize, beans, and squash, they were psychologically geared to accept this new but similar way of obtaining their subsistence. They planted seeds now instead of gathering them.

I called this earliest stage, before agriculture had become established, *The Time of Limited Wandering.* In so far as I can grasp the situation I should be inclined to call it a stable era, one of essentially unchanging continuity. Before agriculture was introduced, the minor changes that took place in the traditional cultural forms did not radically shift the general "slant" of the culture. The old ways of doing things, the traditional forms, persisted over a long period of time (several thousand years perhaps) without great changes.

There were probably contacts with other peoples and cultures, but it is somewhat difficult to document this statement. Perhaps I can point to the beads made from shells which came from the Pacific Ocean; to the distribution by trade of special rocks such as jasper, chalcedony, and obsidian, to be used for blades or projectile points; and to the wide distribution of tubular pipes, to be used for smoking or for curing the sick. I might also add to this list special weaving and woodworking techniques that were widespread in the Desert Culture area and that probably indicate contacts with other people and places.

A TIME OF COMING TOGETHER

The next era, which endured for about 1,500 years and which commenced about 500 B.C., was called *The Emergence of Small Sedentary Communities.* During this time farming was practiced. Maize, beans, and squash were planted regularly. In addition, some wild foods such as yucca pods, cacti, black walnuts, acorns, grass seeds, primrose leaves and sunflower seeds were gathered and were used to supplement the farm products. Architecture and pottery made their appearance during this epoch and many changes resulted from these innovations. These were introduced from without, by contacts.

In spite of the fact that many of the traditional forms, artifacts, and ways of life persisted, one can note tendencies toward elaboration and divergence: alteration of the subsistence pattern through agriculture; introduction of houses and changes in their forms; production of some new artifact types (pottery and metates, bows and arrows, axes); and elaboration of pottery styles and designs, and of ceremonial life.

Contacts with outside groups are marked by the introduction by trade or other forms of social intercourse of many new traits, some of which have been named: agriculture from Mexico; shell bracelets and shell pendants from the Pacific coast; new projectile point forms; reed cigarettes, probably from Mexico; the bow and arrow, probably from Canada; pottery and pottery designs from Mexico; different weaving techniques from the Anasazi; and possibly the ventilator apparatus for small kivas from the Anasazi. In general, during the early part of this stage, contacts and culture change resulted chiefly from trade or other relationships with people to the south; but after about A.D. 500 more and more contacts were made with the Anasazi, to the north. All of these additional traits were fused with those already possessed by the Mogollon Indians. Thus, a different-appearing Mogollon culture was forged, with perhaps Cochise-Mogollon traits and peculiarities dominating.

I should note here that the items I call "trade" are really the results of contacts. From such objects and situations I have made inferences (in the preceding chapters) concerning the behavior of the people by trying to observe the results of innovations on the culture as reflected in material objects and their associations. I have been greatly aided, of course, by

137

the study of similar situations recorded for contemporary Southwestern Indian cultures, notably the Hopi, Zuñi, Pima and Papago.

With all of this fermentation taking place, was this era, from 500 B.C. to A.D. 1000, one of upheaval? In general, yes; I should think that it was unstable from time to time; but I also think that after farming, architecture, and pottery-making had been assimilated there would have been fairly stable periods of several generations or so in length. Of course, the terms "stable" and "unstable" are relative as I use them; they express only difference in degree. In a stable period of a healthy society I should expect some changes.

THE CLIMAX AT PINE LAWN

The last stage, which was very short (A.D. 1000 to 1300 or 1350), I called *The Beginnings of Town Life*. In this brief time, and one that can be looked upon with some sadness, many innovations were noted. Drastic changes in architecture and perhaps in other non-material traditions took place. Many of the contacts that can be observed by means of the material objects and village remains were with the Anasazi Indians to the north and the Hohokam Indians to the west and south.

Anasazi traditions that were taken over include surface rooms arranged in cellular fashion and with masonry walls; black on white pottery bearing Puerco-River-drainage designs; cooking pottery with indented-corrugated necks; full-grooved axes; flint saws; turquoise pendants; and the mealing-bin complex. The traits that came as the result of contacts with peoples to the south and west (Hohokam, probably) are tepary beans, cotton, various "characteristics" of the corn, paint palettes, carved and cut shell, the three quarters-grooved axe, copper bells, and the style of stone carving. Thus there was convergence of Hohokam and Anasazi traditions with those of the Mogollon.

The balance achieved between man and nature permitted a mildly dense population. People tended to cluster in towns of modest size because town life appealed to them for ceremonial and socializing reasons and because their farms could be managed easily enough from this vantage point. Some form of chieftainship or town organization probably existed because the towns were becoming sizable and therefore some mild but central authority would have been needed. At least it seems plausible to assume that common interests and the common weal would have caused submission to a central authority, especially in regard to community building-projects, planting, harvesting, the calendar, and group rituals.

I believe that ideas or people or both peacefully penetrated the Pine Lawn–Reserve and adjacent areas from the north and perhaps from the south. We have no evidence that force was employed to bring about the changes noted. There was no sharp cleavage with the past except for the change in some traditions and the addition of new ones. It should be remembered that traits had been flowing out of and into the Mogollon area for some time and hence there would have been no sharp conflicts.

In spite of the new ways of life and the subsequent convergence or hybridization, most of the older Mogollon traditions such as types of tools, culinary pottery, smudged pottery, and pit-houses continued to thrive lustily. Even the "public" buildings such as the kivas were essentially Mogollon. Hence we have fusion but with a dominance of the older, local Mogollon culture. The villages consisted of enclosed plazas with rooms facing inward, in lieu of the earlier unorganized clusters of rooms.

FATE OF MOGOLLON INDIANS

Here, then, is a long segment of culture history, the beginnings of which were, in pre-agricultural times, flowing through various stages to a final flowering represented by the commencement of town life, well-established agricultural practices, many additions and comforts, and the beginnings of what we can call "civilization." It would be difficult at present to find anywhere in the world such a long-documented developmental and continuous sequence; one that can be traced from a food-gathering–wandering stage to one of established farming communities, covering perhaps some ten to twelve thousand years of unbroken existence. We are fortunate in having this history for study.

The material results of all of this have been published, but it will take a long time for the significance of these researches to be thoroughly exploited and tied up to the story of the history of civilization. I have merely skimmed the surface; the bulk is yet there to be digested and formulated in general laws and in a philosophy concerning man and his will to progress, no matter what obstacles are put in his path, and perhaps the "spontaneous" development of civilization.

We can demonstrate by means of our data that we have unearthed and pieced together a cultural continuum in which man's development was slow, but steady and progressive. Progress—an ill-used word—but progress, no matter what definition is used, was attained. Man progressed by exerting a small bit of control over natural forces. He controlled his environment to a limited extent by selective breeding of races of corn and by planting it and beans and squash and thus assuring himself of a stable food supply.

If he had progressed, why did he not continue to do so? What halted the Mogollon Indians and what became of them? There are several answers to these questions. The matter is not a simple one.

First of all, as far as we can make out, the Mogollon culture at about A.D. 1300 or 1400 had retained its Mogollon "slant" and vigor and was still going strong when it ran headlong into insurmountable obstacles.

The Mogollon Indians, even if they had remained in the area I have been discussing, could probably not have attained the degree of urbanization and civilization that the Mayas, Toltecs, and Aztecs had reached, because the country and the climate were marginal and were not suitable or favorable for great concentrations of population. To have developed much farther on the long road to civilization, a far denser population would have been necessary. The Pine Lawn–Reserve area could not have supported a dense population because: (1) the rainfall was insufficient for big farming projects; (2) there were no water resources that could have been

140

used for irrigation purposes; and (3) the topography was too hilly and rocky to be economically exploited for agriculture unless terracing had been employed. Even then, terraces would have been ineffective without rain or irrigation. Hence, I conclude that the Mogollon Indians had progressed about as far as they ever could have gone. I grant, that if they had not been forced to abandon the area, and if they had remained there many more centuries, and if they had maintained contacts and trade relations with the higher culture centers in Mexico, they might have reached higher cultural plateaus. But they would have had to develop more social co-ordination, more managerial authority, and more craft specialization. Unfortunately, after A.D. 1350 or 1400, many of the Mexican cultures had collapsed, and thus stimuli from this area would not have been forthcoming.

But the Mogollon Indians did not remain in their homeland. Drought, the beginnings of enemy (Apache?) raids, extinction of certain clans, making impossible the celebration of certain ceremonies, or other as yet undiscovered reasons forced a hegira. They gradually abandoned their homeland of many centuries and moved out. By A.D. 1400 at the latest, they had disappeared. Apache or other Indians may have camped in the area from time to time, but not until the coming of the white settlers in the mid-nineteenth century were there any permanent settlers and farmers. At present, we are exploring the trail of the Mogollones as they dispersed south, west, and north. It is hoped that eventually we may discover where they went. On the basis of present evidence, I guess that some of them moved west and north. It is possible that descendants of these Mogollones are living today at Zuñi.

DEVELOPMENT OF MOGOLLON CULTURE

Now I return to the statement, made at the outset of this chapter, that I was interested in seeking explanations and causes of how and why the Mogollon culture developed. I stated then that the significant causes elude me. I have only a few superficial explanations to set forth, some of which have already been alluded to in this chapter.

In their earliest stage we saw the Mogollon Indians or their ancestors living a simple life that was devoted principally to satisfying the basic biological needs for food, shelter, and clothing. These needs were obtained by fundamental technologies such as tool-making, manufacture of weapons and traps, weaving, and a knowledge of what plants were edible, where they grew, and when their fruits were ripe. This stage was reached by many peoples in various parts of the world at a very early time. Some peoples never passed beyond this stage, partly because they did not have the opportunity, partly because they lacked the stimulation from others, and partly because they were indifferent to other traditions and ways of life. Sometimes a new idea will be rejected by people and the exact reason for this is unknown.

In the next stage we noted great advances among the Mogollones. The idea of planting and cultivating corn, squash, and beans was borrowed from people to the south; or possibly they were stimulated by the visits of traders from Mexico to adopt this brilliant idea of obtaining security in food supplies by planting and cultivating crops. If the Mogollon Indians had lived in a barren desert, agriculture would not have been possible. Hence, they were fortunate in inhabiting a well-watered area that facilitated the adoption of the idea; and they were fortunate in having developed food-gathering habits that required them to pay great attention to plant life and nurture. In gathering plants and preparing them for flour-cookery the Mogollones had at hand digging sticks (formerly used for digging up plants, but now to be used in tilling the ground for planting seeds), collecting baskets, and various kinds of milling stones and mortars and pestles. Thus, at hand were the necessary implements and techniques for practicing agriculture.

Then, by means of communications and contacts, other traits were borrowed by the Mogollones, notably pit-houses and pottery-making. The pattern of Mogollon culture took form at this time and remained largely unchanged for many centuries. We can probably visualize this stage as one in which population increased; in which the culture of the peoples expanded; in which there was little danger of wars; and in which many stimulations were received from other peoples, especially those inhabiting Mexico.

The final stages of this culture were marked by efflorescence of the traits at hand, and the appearance of several new ones. There were no additions to the basic technologies and no inventions. Population increased as agriculture became better understood and was more efficiently practiced. An increase in food supply permitted some people to have more leisure for developing the arts and crafts and for enriching the intellectual and ceremonial life.

WHAT BLOCKED FURTHER DEVELOPMENT

Thus Mogollon folk had reached an apogee for them, a stage midway between a primitive pre-agricultural era and civilization. It was fated that they could go no farther. The reasons for this were suggested earlier in this section. To provide a deeper explanation of even their limited development can not be done at the moment. Certainly some of the factors were a semi-arid environment that facilitated the growth of culture, and access to many stimuli from a region of several diversified higher cultures (Mexico). If the Mogollon folk had been cut off from contacts with various peoples possessing higher cultures, it is doubtful if they would have progressed as far as they did.

Various obstacles—terrain, rainfall, some isolation—prevented the formation of large communities integrated through control by a theocracy with centralized authority, the accumulation of surpluses, and the development of intense specialization, metallurgy, large-scale trade, writing, mathematics, irrigation, and a subsequent upsurge in population. All of these factors appear to be necessary attributes and ingredients of higher civilizations, and all were lacking in the Mogollon culture. Since the creation and development of these conditions were impossibilities, we have here one explanation for the limited growth of this culture.

But the basic explanation of why peoples rise above "savagery," and why they spontaneously develop even limited civilization like the Mogollon, is yet to be discovered.

143

We hope that the detailed knowledge of the Mogollon culture and its rise and migration will contribute to a methodology that will suggest "laws" as to why particular cultures develop, and that this in turn will throw light on contemporary as well as future events.

VALUE of

ARCHAEOLOGY

MEANING AND USES OF ARCHAEOLOGY

Some newspaper articles have led the public to think that archaeological excavations are conducted solely for the purpose of removing valuable objects or treasures from the earth by haphazard digging. Actually, archaeological work is an effort to reconstruct the history and characteristics of a bygone period; to make reasonable conjectures that are inferred from a small body of materials gathered by excavations; and to guess about what is missing from what has survived.

Archaeology, then, gathers the material remnants of a past civilization—tools, pottery, and cast-off objects—and makes these things live again. Archaeologists collect and classify, and then make speculations concerning the things classified so that this knowledge may be of help to us in understanding our own times and our own problems. We learn from the past collective experience of societies long dead; we build on the past.

The archaeologist digs carefully and observingly layer on layer and brings everything except the dirt home to the laboratory for analysis because he is unable in the field to judge what is important and what is not.

The excavating is done carefully, because most of the history of the site is contained in the earth that lies over and on it. The "history" is gleaned not from surviving written records— for there are none in most instances—but from the painstaking archaeological work.

To tear an object from its resting place without first gathering all necessary data and without taking photographs is like ripping a page from a valuable book. If the object is cleaned and placed on a shelf without its genealogy it is useless and mute. It can tell us little or nothing. The object is not important for itself but it becomes invaluable if we know its "associates," that is, the conditions under which it was found and the other things that were found with it.

We are forced to use only material objects because in most instances nothing else remains for us to study. We try to interpret the uses of these objects in the life of the people who made them. How widely were they distributed and over how long a period of time were they used? Can we trace the development of different kinds of housing and tools? Can we discover the laws that govern the development of peoples in similar climates of the world? We try to analyze and compare the similarities and parallels in these developments because we are seeking explanations for similarities and are trying to find out if there are laws that govern the rise and fall of civilizations.

In striving to reach an explanation of the causes of these similar developments and of their effects, we attempt to establish some general principles. For example, an increased population must have an increased food supply, and in an arid region this can be secured only by irrigation, which therefore must be developed if the group is to grow or if it does not wish to split and emigrate.

Writing is an example of a similar and a parallel development found in both the Old and the New World. Writing appeared independently and spontaneously in the eastern and western hemispheres after the people who had devised it had developed similar basic technologies and irrigation.

But, as mentioned above, interpretation of our material is often difficult, for we have only cast-off, broken objects to work with, often few in number and strange in appearance. Sometimes, if we are fortunate, we find a cave that has been occupied for several thousand years and that has been bone dry during all of that time. The dryness preserves all those perishable objects—cloth, sandals, wooden objects, skins, agricultural products—that would rot if left in an open site. Thus we acquire important material that is valuable in attempting to reconstruct the way of life of the inhabitants of the region.

As I have indicated, digging is usually done under adverse conditions—dust, mud, rain, heat, insects. There is little glamour involved. Nevertheless, there is a zest about digging, arduous though it is, or we would not do it. We may dig for weeks without finding more than bits of charcoal or a few broken pieces of pottery.

IMPORTANCE OF ARCHAEOLOGY OF THE NEW WORLD

At this point, my reader may say: "Very well. The Greeks and Romans contributed to our civilization; but what is the good of investigating Indian cultures?"

My answer is twofold: The American Indians have contributed to our way of life by giving us ideas in architecture (Pueblo and Maya) and by giving us many valuable food plants such as potatoes, tomatoes, peanuts, corn, beans, squash (to name only a few).

The second part of my answer is slightly more involved. We should be glad to investigate Indian civilizations, even if we assumed that they had contributed nothing to ours, because America and the Indians were pretty much cut off from the Old World and the differing cultures were developed here more or less independently, after the Indians (Mongoloid peoples) had emigrated here via Siberia. In short, the New World constitutes a kind of gigantic test tube, a great laboratory where all sorts of events were taking place, with few or only occasional influences seeping into the New from the Old World. This is one of the few such "laboratories" that we know of, since it is impossible to place societies in a test tube and watch what happens. Most anthropologists believe that the achievements of the Indians were independently developed in the New World. These achievements rested on a few basic traits that the Indians brought with them: pressure flaking; grinding bone, horn and stone; hafting tools; weaving baskets, mats, and fish weirs; making cordage; making fire; propelling projectiles from a spear thrower; and using a domesticated animal—the dog. In looking over this short list of the traits brought with them and by comparing it with what the Indian had accomplished up to 1492, we can see that remarkable progress had been made.

If the major achievements were independently evolved— and the weight of evidence appears on this side—and if we can find parallels in achievements, similarities in developments, or any regularities of occurrences in both hemispheres then we may be able to organize our information so that we can begin to look for relationships between causes and effects. In short, we may be able to discover why civilizations wax and wane.

Many well-known achievements apparently developed independently in the Old and New Worlds: domestication of plants and animals; irrigation; increase of population and growth of towns and cities; elaborate social groupings into priesthoods, states, and empires; development of pottery; production of weaving and metal-working; invention of writing, mathematics, and calendars; production of painting, sculpture, temple palaces, pyramids, and tombs. These are a few examples of similar and parallel developments, of "cultural regularities."

In all the semi-arid early centers of civilization, man started as a user of crude tools of stone and a hunter or a food-gatherer, and from 4,000 to 9,000 years later he had become a "civilized" creature who had devised, discovered, invented, and evolved all the basic traits and institutions that I have just listed.

I am not saying that all men have passed through parallel, unrelated stages; nor am I saying that there are necessarily universal stages in development that apply to all cultures; nor again, that the sequences of development are universal. But I do say that undoubtedly there are a number of important basic independent parallels that may be explained by the independent operation of identical causes, provided the comparisons are restricted to comparable groups. It would make no sense to compare the Hottentots, the Eskimos, and the Egyptians.

If a civilization is balanced and if all the elements of the culture are in harmony—that is, the ratio, for example, of agriculture to hunting and gathering, to artistic and religious expressions—then the chances are that the civilization will be a sound and happy one. If any one element or if any one philosophy of the culture becomes more important or if emphases of the culture are shifted to a false evaluation (such as dictators, racism, conquests), then that civilization may be doomed. This may be one answer as to why several great civilizations have perished in the past. I would hazard a guess that our primitive Mogollon Indians, living in their caves, or later in their pit-houses, or still later in their apartment dwellings, probably lived a happier life and perhaps a somewhat better one than did the Maya Indians with all their arts and crafts, and all their skill in building and in mathematics, for eventually something in the Maya civilization became unbalanced. Of course you can come right back at me and say, "Well what happened to the Mogollon Indians? Why didn't their civilization continue if it was so well balanced and such a happy one?" That is a fair question but I cannot answer it specifically at this moment. In the preceding chapter of this book I have tried to explain our theories or conjectures concerning the apparent "disappearance" of the Mogollon civilization and what probably happened to these people.

And so the value of archaeology lies in developing a new way of looking at life, in searching for truth and beauty where it leads us, and in helping us understand our times and our problems. We need to broaden our understanding of man's hopes and desires and our knowledge of man's nature. Perhaps if all of us put our heads together we can discover the causes for the rise and decline of civilizations and perhaps save our own from disappearing.

Bibliography

Aveleyra A. de Anda, Luis
1956. Second mammoth and associated artifacts at Santa Isabel Izto-pan, Mexico. American Antiquity, vol. 22, no. 1, pp. 12–28.

Broecker, W. S., and Kulp, W. S.
1956. Radiocarbon method of age determination. American Antiq-uity, vol. 22, no. 1, pp. 1–11.

Carpenter, Rhys
1933. Humanistic value of archaeology. Harvard University Press.

Collier, Donald
1951. New radiocarbon method for dating the past. Chicago Natural History Museum Bulletin, vol. 22, no. 1, pp. 6–7.

Covarrubias, Miguel
1954. The eagle, the jaguar, and the serpent. Origins of the American Indian, chap. I, pp. 9–23. Alfred A. Knopf, New York.

Cutler, Hugh C.
1951. The oldest corn in the world. Chicago Natural History Museum Bulletin, vol. 22, no. 2, pp. 4–5.

Douglass, A. E.
1929. The secret of the southwest solved by talkative tree rings. National Geographic Magazine, vol. 56, no. 6, pp. 736–770.

Dozier, Edward P.
1954. The Hopi-Tewa of Arizona. University of California Publica-tions in Archaeology and Ethnology, vol. 44, no. 3, pp. 259–376.

Eggan, Fred
1950. Social organization of the western pueblos. University of Chicago Press.

Eiseley, Loren C.
See Meggers, Betty, and Evans, Clifford

151

FRANKFORT, HENRI
  1956. The birth of civilization in the Near East. Doubleday Anchor Books, Garden City, New York.

HARRINGTON, M. R.
  1954. The oldest camp-fires. The Masterkey, vol. 28, no. 6, pp. 233–234. Los Angeles, California.
  1955. A new Tule Springs expedition. The Masterkey, vol. 29, no. 4, pp. 112–114. Los Angeles, California.

HAURY, EMIL W.
  1936. The Mogollon culture of southwestern New Mexico. The Medallion Papers, nos. 19 and 20, Gila Pueblo, Globe, Arizona.
  1940. Excavations in the Forestdale Valley, east-central Arizona. University of Arizona Bulletin, vol. 11, no. 4.
  1955. Artifacts with mammoth remains, Naco, Arizona. American Antiquity, vol. 19, no. 1, pp. 1–14.

HAURY, EMIL W., and SAYLES, E. B.
  1947. An early pit house village of the Mogollon culture. University of Arizona Bulletin, vol. 18, no. 4.

HOUGH, WALTER
  1907. Antiquities of the upper Gila and Salt River valleys in Arizona and New Mexico. Smithsonian Institution, Bureau of American Ethnology, Bulletin 35.

HOWELLS, WILLIAM
  1954. Back of history. The oldest Americans, chap. 17, pp. 273–290. Doubleday & Company, New York.

JENNINGS, JESSE D.
  1957. Danger Cave. American Antiquity, vol. 23, no. 2, part 2.

JENNINGS, JESSE D., and NORBECK, EDWARD
  1955. Great Basin prehistory: A review. American Antiquity, vol. 21, no. 1, pp. 1–11.

KRIEGER, ALEX D.
  1953. Anthropology today. *Editor and Chairman*, A. L. KROEBER. New World culture history: Anglo-America, pp. 238–264. University of Chicago Press.

LA FARGE, OLIVER
  1956. Pictorial history of the American Indian, pp. 11–25. Crown Publishers, Inc., New York.

LIBBY, WILLARD F.
  1955. Radiocarbon dating. University of Chicago Press.

McGREGOR, JOHN C.
  1941. Southwestern archaeology. Dendrochronology, chap. 5. John Willey and Sons, Inc., New York.

MANGELSDORF, PAUL C., and SMITH, C. EARLE, JR.
1949. New archaeological evidence on evolution in maize. Harvard University, Botanical Museum Leaflets, vol. 13, no. 8.

MARTIN, PAUL S.
1940. The SU site. Excavations at a Mogollon village, western New Mexico. Field Museum of Natural History, Anthropological Series, vol. 32, no. 1.
1943. The SU site. Excavations at a Mogollon village, western New Mexico. Field Museum of Natural History, Anthropological Series, vol. 32, no. 2.
1957. Glottochronology: Dating by words. Chicago Natural History Museum Bulletin, vol. 28, no. 5, pp. 2, 7.

MARTIN, P. S., QUIMBY, G. I., and COLLIER, DONALD
1947. Indians before Columbus. Origin of the American Indians, chap. 2, pp. 15–22. University of Chicago Press.

MARTIN, P. S., and RINALDO, JOHN B.
1946. The SU site. Excavations at a Mogollon village, western New Mexico. Field Museum of Natural History, Anthropological Series, vol. 32, no. 3.
1950a. Turkey Foot Ridge site. A Mogollon village, Pine Lawn Valley, western New Mexico. Fieldiana: Anthropology, vol. 38, no. 2.
1950b. Sites of the Reserve Phase, Pine Lawn Valley, western New Mexico. Fieldiana: Anthropology, vol. 38, no. 3.
1951. The Southwestern co-tradition. Southwestern Journal of Anthropology, vol. 7, no. 3, pp. 215–229.

MARTIN, P. S., RINALDO, J. B., and ANTEVS, ERNST
1949. Cochise and Mogollon sites, Pine Lawn Valley, western New Mexico. Fieldiana: Anthropology, vol. 38, no. 1.

MARTIN, P. S., RINALDO, J. B., and BLUHM, E.
1954. Caves of the Reserve Area. Fieldiana: Anthropology, vol. 42.

MARTIN, P. S., RINALDO, J. B., BLUHM, E., and CUTLER, H. C.
1956. Higgins Flat Pueblo, western New Mexico. Fieldiana: Anthropology, vol. 45.

MARTIN, P. S., RINALDO, J. B., BLUHM, ELAINE, CUTLER, H. C., and GRANGE, ROGER, JR.
1952. Mogollon cultural continuity and change: The stratigraphic analysis of Tularosa and Cordova caves. Fieldiana: Anthropology, vol. 40.

MEGGERS, BETTY, and EVANS, CLIFFORD (Editors)
1955. New interpretations of aboriginal American culture history. The Palaeo Indians: Their survival and diffusion, pp. 1–11, by LOREN C. EISELEY. Anthropological Society of Washington, Washington, D.C.

MULLER, HERBERT J.
1957. The uses of the past. Oxford University Press.
1958. The loom of history. Harper and Brothers, New York.

MURDOCK, GEORGE P.
1949. Social structure. The MacMillan Company, New York.

RINALDO, J. B., and BLUHM, E.
1956. Late Mogollon pottery types of the Reserve Area. Fieldiana: Anthropology, vol. 36, no. 7.

SAPIR, EDWARD
1939. Language. Harcourt, Brace and Company, New York.

SAYLES, E. B.
1945. The San Simon Branch excavations at Cave Creek and in the San Simon Valley. I. Material culture. Medallion Papers, no. 34, Gila Pueblo, Globe, Arizona.

SAYLES, E. B., and ANTEVS, ERNST
1941. The Cochise culture. Medallion Papers, no. 29, Gila Pueblo, Globe, Arizona.

SMILEY, TERAH L.
1952. A summary of tree-ring dates from some Southwestern archaeological sites. University of Arizona Bulletin, vol. 22, no. 4, pp. 1–32.
1955. Geochronology. University of Arizona Bulletin, vol. 26, no. 2, pp. 1–200.

STEWARD, JULIAN H.
1938. Basin-Plateau aboriginal sociopolitical groups. Smithsonian Institution, Bureau of American Ethnology, Bulletin 120.
1949. Cultural causality and law: A trial formulation of the development of early civilizations. American Anthropologist, vol. 51, no. 1, pp. 1–27.
1955. Irrigation civilizations: A comparative study. Pan American Union, Washington, D.C.

STEWARD, JULIAN H., COLLIER, DONALD, et al.
1955. Irrigation civilizations: a comparative study. Social Science Monographs I, Pan American Union, Washington, D.C. pp. 1–78.

TITIEV, MISCHA
1954. The science of man. Man and culture in the New World, part I, chap. 16, pp. 273–297. Henry Holt & Company, New York.

UNDERHILL, RUTH
1941. The northern Paiute Indians of California and Nevada. Department of the Interior, Bureau of Indian Affairs.

WAUCHOPE, ROBERT, and OTHERS
1956. Seminars in archaeology: 1955. Society for American Archaeology, Memoirs, no. 11, pp. 61–110.

WHEAT, JOE BEN
1954. Crooked Ridge Village. University of Arizona Bulletin, vol. 25, no. 3, pp. 1–183.

Index